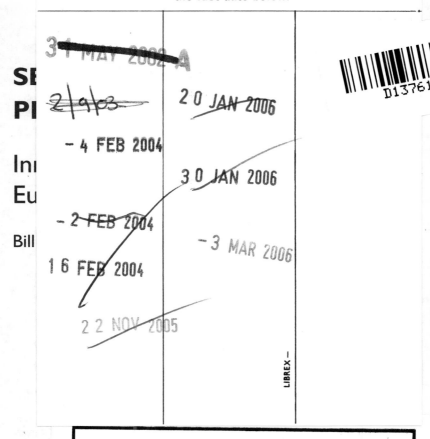

SE
Pl

In
Eu

Bill

The POLICY

PP

P R E S S

J C S H R

FEANTSA

First published in Great Britain in 1999 by

The Policy Press
University of Bristol
34 Tyndall's Park Road
Bristol BS8 1PY
UK
Tel no +44 (0)117 954 6800
Fax no +44 (0)117 973 7308
E-mail tpp@bristol.ac.uk
http://www.bristol.ac.uk/Publications/TPP/

ISBN 1 86134 189 X

Bill Edgar and **Joe Doherty** are Directors of the Joint Centre for Scottish Housing Research at the University of Dundee and the University of St Andrews. **Amy Mina-Coull** is a Research Associate at the Centre.

This research was made possible thanks to the financial support of DG V of the European Commission, through FEANTSA, and the participation of the research institutes and universities as part of the European Observatory on Homelessness.

Cover design by Qube Design Associates, Bristol.
Printed in Great Britain by Hobbs the Printers Ltd, Southampton.

Contents

List of figures and tables

Figures

Tables

Foreword

Recent demographic changes, high unemployment, and changes in family life have all, of course, had repercussions on the composition of the population of those we describe as having 'no fixed abode' and also on the means and the methods employed by public services and non-governmental organisations (NGOs) in the European Union.

It is therefore important work which has been carried out by the research correspondents of the European Observatory on Homelessness and by the team of the Joint Centre for Scottish Housing Research (JCSHR) who have succeeded in putting together a particularly illuminating report.

I would especially like to thank the authors of this transnational report for having addressed methodological and sociological problems in ways that can be readily understood by service providers and by decision makers and for having succeeded in clearly analysing the major trends that can be seen in all our countries, while recognising the diversity that exists in terms of legislative, regulatory, historical and even cultural differences.

Some trends are becoming evident, such as the greater adaptation of services to the individual and to the needs of specific groups; the decentralisation of policies and the creation of local and regional networks of services; and finally – and this strikes me as an especially positive development – the provision of housing as part of an integrated strategy for the social inclusion of those with 'no fixed abode'.

The report also draws attention to the capacity for innovation which has been demonstrated by those with responsibility for tackling homelessness. This must encourage us to continue our efforts in terms of research and the exchange of experiences. By means of networking among our members, who represent a vast wealth of know-how and creativity, and through our collective capacity to engage in fruitful dialogue with political decision makers in our countries and also at EU level, the Fédération Européenne D'Associations Nationales Travaillant avec les Sans-Abri (FEANTSA) has, without doubt, contributed towards the 'quiet revolution' in services which is described by this report.

I hope that this report will provide encouragement to everyone who is concerned with addressing the needs of the growing numbers of homeless people. I particularly wish to thank our partners: the 15 research institutes of the Observatory, and the European Commission (DGV – Social Affairs) for their support which has enabled us, as in previous years, to realise and to publish this report.

Michel Mercadié
President of FEANTSA

Acknowledgements

Our primary debt is to the national corespondents of the European
Observatory on Homelessness. Their national reports provide the
empirical basis for this report and were instrumental in sparking our
ideas for the analytical framework. We therefore acknowledge our debt
and extend our thanks to the following correspondents: Robert Aldridge
(UK), Tobias Børner Stax and Ingrid Koch-Nielson (Denmark), Alfredo
Bruto da Costa (Portugal), Volker Busch-Geertsema (Germany), Pascal
de Decker (Belgium), Henk de Feijter (Netherlands), Anne de Gouy
(France), Sirkka-Liisa Kärkkäinen and Laura Hassi (Finland), Angelika
Kofler (Austria), Jesús Leal Maldonado and T. Lainez Romano (Spain),
Eoin O'Sullivan (Ireland), Monique Pels (Luxembourg), Ingrid Sahlin
(Sweden), Aristides Sapounakis (Greece) and Antonio Tosi (Italy).

We would also like to acknowledge the contribution of Mary Daly
and Jan Vranken, members of FEANTSA's Scientific Committee, as
well as the key roles played by Catherine Parmentier and John Evans at
FEANTSA in coordinating the project and in organising the annual
meetings of the Observatory correspondents in Brussels, meetings which
provided a crucial forum for the exchange of ideas and the clarification
of concepts. We would also like to express our thanks to Dawn Pudney
of The Policy Press for her consistent good humour and impressive
efficiency in bringing this book to speedy publication.

FEANTSA and the European Observatory on Homelessness

FEANTSA (the European Federation of National Organisations working with the homeless) is an international non-governmental organisation founded in 1989. FEANTSA has more than 50 members drawn from the European Union and other European countries. FEANTSA's remit is to engage in dialogue with European institutions and national governments in order to promote the development and implementation of effective measures to tackle the causes of homelessness. FEANTSA receives funding from the European Commission, is supported by the European Parliament and has consultative status at the Council of Europe.

The European Observatory on Homelessness was set up by FEANTSA in 1991 to conduct research into homelessness in Europe. It is composed of a network of national correspondents who collect information concerning homelessness and other relevant policy measures in the EU member states. Each year the Observatory produces a series of national reports on specific research themes and these are published as a European Report analysing transnational trends. The research of the Observatory is supported financially by DGV of the European Commission.

Contact address: FEANTSA, 1 rue Defacqz, B-1000 Brussels, Belgium. Tel 32/2/538 66 69; Fax 32/2/539 41 74; e-mail feantsa@compuserve.com; Website: www.feantsa.org

Coordinators and correspondents of the European Observatory on Homelessness: 1998-99

Coordinators

Bill Edgar, Co-Director of the Joint Centre for Scottish Housing Research, School of Town and Regional Planning, University of Dundee, Dundee DD1 4HT, UK Tel (44) (0)1382 345238; e-mail w.m.edgar@dundee.ac.uk

Joe Doherty, Co-Director of the Joint Centre for Scottish Housing Research, School of Geography and Geosciences, University of St Andrews, St Andrews, Fife KY16 9ST, UK Tel (44) (0)1334 463911; e-mail jd@st-andrews.ac.uk

Amy Mina-Coull, Research Associate of the Joint Centre for Scottish Housing Research.

National correspondents

Austria: Angelika Kofler, Research Fellow, Interdisciplinary Centre for Comparative Research in the Social Sciences, Hamburgerstrasse 14/20, A-1050 Vienna Tel (43) 587 3973; Fax (43) 1587 397310; e-mail a.kofler@iccr.co.at

Belgium: Pascal de Decker, Cabinet of Flemish Minister of Internal Affairs, Urban Policy and Housing, Gent Tel (32) 121 227 2527; Fax (32) 191 220 5926; e-mail pascal.de.decker@skynet.be

Denmark: Tobias Børner Stax and Inge Koch Nielson, The Danish National Institute of Social Science, Herluf Trolles Gade 11, DK-1052, Copenhagen K Tel (45) 3348 0860; e-mail Tob@sfi.dk

Finland: Sirkka-Liisa Kärkkäinen, STAKES, Pl 200, Fl-00531, Helsinki Tel (358) 19 13967 2068; Fax (358) 19 13967 2054; e-mail sirkkali@stakes3.stakes.fi

France: Anne de Gouy, Director General, Association Habitat Educatif, 101 rue Talma, 94 400 Vitry sur Seine Tel (33) 1 46 82 38 02; Fax (33) 1 46 82 38 55

Germany: Volker Busch-Geertsema, Senior Researcher, GISS [Association for Innovative Social Research and Social Planning], Kohlhoekerstrasse 22, D-28203 Bremen Tel (49) 421 339 8833; Fax (49) 421 339 8835; e-mail giss-bremen@t-online.de

Greece: Aristides Sapounakis, Lecturer, Department of Planning and Peripheral Development, University of Thessaly Tel (30) 177 03 357; Fax (30) 177 10 816; e-mail arsapkiv@mail.hol.gr

Ireland: Eoin O'Sullivan, Department of Social Studies, Trinity College, Dublin 2 Tel (353) 1 608 2548; Fax (353) 1 671 2262; e-mail tosullivan@tcd.ie

Italy: Antonio Tosi, Dipartmento di Scienze del Territorio, Politecnico Milan, Via Bonardi 3, 20133 Milan Tel (39) 121 2399 5417; Fax (39) 121 2399 5435

Luxembourg: Monique Pels, CEPS/INSTEAD, BP 48 L-4501 Differdange Tel (352) 58 5855 536; Fax (352) 58 5560

Netherlands: Henk de Feijter, Planologisch demograpfisch institut, University of Amsterdam, Nieuwe Prinsengracht 130, NL-1018 VZ Amsterdam Tel (31) 20 525 4640; Fax (31) 20 525 4041; e-mail H.J.Feijter@frw.uva.nl

Portugal: Alfredo Bruto da Costa, Portuguese Catholic University, rua Eiffel 4, 3° Esq Lisbon Tel (351) 1796 8944; Fax (351) 1795 1835; e-mail alfredo.bc@mail.telepac.pt

Spain: Jesús Leal Maldonado, Faculty of Political Sciences and Sociology, Universidad Complutense de Madrid, Campus de Somosaguas, E-28023 Madrid Tel (34) 111 394 2644; Fax (34) 111 394 2646; e-mail 5050204@sis.vcm.es

Sweden: Ingrid Sahlin, Department of Sociology, Lund University, PO Box 114, S-221 Lund Tel (46) 462 22 4748; Fax (46) 462 22 4794; e-mail Ingrid.Sahlin@soc.lu.se

United Kingdom: Robert Aldridge, Scottish Council for the Single Homeless, Wellgate House, 200 Cowgate, Edinburgh EH1 1NQ UK Tel (44) 131 2264 382; Fax (44) 131 2254 382; e-mail Robert@scsh.co.uk

ONE

Introduction

This study examines the changing nature of service provision for the homeless in Europe with a particular focus on the emergence of new and innovative projects and programmes. Over recent decades Europe has experienced profound economic and demographic change which has been manifest, inter alia, in sustained high levels of unemployment and the deconstruction of traditional family structures. Such transformations have contributed to both a rise in the levels of homelessness and to a change in the composition of the homeless population across all European countries. These increases and changes have, particularly in the context of increasingly stringent controls on public expenditure, placed unprecedented demands on and frequently called into question the viability of many of the established forms of service provision for homeless people. Challenges to the efficacy of existing service provision have created the conditions for the emergence of new and innovative initiatives which attempt to address in a more effective manner the changed circumstances and changed needs of Europe's homeless population.

This report is based in part on national reports from the 15 correspondents of the European Observatory on Homelessness. The brief of these correspondents was to select, on the basis of their research, examples of innovative services for the homeless in their respective countries (see the case study summaries in the Appendix). For the purpose of this exercise, innovative services were defined as those which *'aim at achieving reintegration of homeless people by means of new approaches to individuals and practices which differ from mainstream forms of assistance'*. This definition reflected a working hypothesis, which the correspondents were asked to bear in mind, that innovative schemes which moved the focus from institutional living to an individualised approach to reintegration offer a more effective way of bridging the gap between the provision of emergency assistance and the attainment of permanent housing; successful innovations are those which achieve integration and prevent lapsing back into homelessness. The correspondents were also asked to place their analysis of innovative services in a national social and political context, in particular, to relate service provision for the homeless to the evolution of the welfare state in their respective countries.

Concepts of homelessness

There is, at present, no single or consistent definition of homelessness which is accepted and applied by policy makers and researchers throughout the European community. The absence of an agreed definition makes comparative study of the nature, causes and impact of homelessness difficult. In this study of innovation and change in the provision of services for the homeless we need to be aware of the nature of this variation and of the problems in arriving at an operational definition.

In some countries, Britain for example, the term homelessness is incorporated into legislation and has a specific definition related to the implementation of statutory duties. However, legally based definitions tend to be narrowly selective, identifying only priority cases, and leaving out important sections of the population who are without a home. It is also evident that social work, health and other professionals do not work with definitions derived from housing legislation.

Some commentators define homelessness in relation to housing conditions (Greve et al, 1986), and in this way identify housing situations which have as their common feature a 'lack of a right or access to a secure and minimally adequate housing space'. These housing situations have variously been described (Johnson et al, 1991; Avramov, 1996a) as rooflessness (living rough), houselessness (relying on emergency accommodation or long-term institutions), or inadequate housing (including insecure accommodation, intolerable housing conditions or involuntary sharing).

However, for others the lack of a dwelling also reflects the absence of social relations and networks and in this context it is important to distinguish between *house*lessness, defined in relation to a person's housing situation and *home*lessness, defined in relation to a person's social situation (Kärkkäinen and Hassi, 1998). As Tosi has argued,

> ... of those principles that order the multiplicity of notions of homelessness, the most obvious is the polarisation around two principal meanings: on the one hand lack of space – a shelter – and on the other hand the absence of social relations

or ties which in turn would reveal situations of social exclusion or marginalisation. (Tosi, 1997a, p 5)

These two notions raise different but related questions: the first raises the general problem of the connections between poverty and housing, and the second, the question of those types and processes of social exclusion that are exacerbated by the loss of housing.

Elsewhere in the literature, homelessness has been characterised as a socially and historically determined concept (Watson, 1984). In this perspective, some groups in society who suffer unequal treatment in the housing market as a result of exclusion may also suffer from poverty as a result of exclusion from the labour market, and experience discrimination on account of their gender, ethnicity, disability or sexual orientation. Additionally, single people suffer particular problems due to "the ideological acceptance of the family norm and by the lack of coherence of non-family and single households as a group" (Watson and Austerberry, 1986). The fact that homelessness policies, with some exceptions, tend to be family centred has, it has been argued, particular implications for single women (Watson, 1984).

From this brief review of some of the literature it can be seen that the meaning of homelessness is fluid and sometimes elusive (Daly, 1999); it is subject to change and adjustment over time and space; it is, in this sense, a relational rather than an absolute concept. From an initial restrictive definition as rooflessness, the concept has developed to embrace notions of risk and causality and is now commonly identified as a facet of social exclusion. Vranken (1997), in considering such variation and changes in the conception of homelessness, asks whether such changes indicate a shift in perspective or paradigm and if this is the case, does this paradigm shift reflect a change in the socioeconomic and demographic composition of the homeless or in the nature of homelessness itself? Or does it simply reflect a development in the academic and policy understanding of homelessness? We would argue that in the context of contemporary Europe it reflects both these tendencies. In this report, which examines the development of innovative services for homeless people, it can be seen that the conceptualisation of homelessness has a clear influence on the types of services provided, the access to those services and the ethos of the legal and administrative procedures which governments may develop to facilitate change and lead to more permanent and effective solutions.

Homelessness and service provision

The European Observatory on Homelessness (which has been researching homelessness in the member states on behalf of FEANTSA since 1991) has presented a general picture of the situation in the 15 European Union (EU) countries. Approximately 3 million people have no fixed home of their own, while a further 15 million people live in sub-standard or overcrowded accommodation (FEANTSA, 1995). In other words, one person in every hundred can actually be described as homeless on any particular night, while something like a further 4% of the population are denied access to decent housing.

Detailed descriptions of the nature and extent of homelessness in Europe and of the characteristics of homeless people is well documented elsewhere (FEANTSA, 1995; Avramov, 1998). For our purposes, it is sufficient here to note three key issues, which have a bearing on research on the development of innovative services. First, based on the evidence of homelessness trends throughout Europe, the problems of homelessness, of housing exclusion, are proving to be persistent and resistant to historic or traditional solutions. Second, the evidence would suggest that there has indeed been a change in the demographic composition of the people using services for the homeless. Finally, in developing effective innovative services, it is important to understand the processes by which homelessness may occur and not just its impact, and to understand the nature of these processes at an individual as well as a structural level.

In this context, Avramov's distinction between structural causes, intermediate causes and proximate (or personal) causes provides a useful perspective. Consideration of structural causes, Avramov (1995) argues, will reveal how the organisation of society may exclude particular groups from access to housing, while intermediate causes tell us which specific population sub-groups are most exposed to the risks of homelessness. The proximate causes demonstrate which individuals in the risk group have the highest risk of homelessness. To the extent that this perspective, while recognising the personal, individual nature of homelessness, focuses on the structural causes of homelessness and embraces notions of social exclusion, it provides a sound basis for developing an understanding of the changing and increasingly multi-faceted nature of homelessness in the EU.

The impact of homelessness needs to be perceived in terms of its duration and in terms of when it occurs in relation to the stage in an individual's life-course. Clearly the objective and focus of services for homeless people should reflect these issues if they are to be effective in their preventative role. For example, the development of innovative services targeted at young single people (at an initial household formation stage of a person's life-course) may, in recognition of the different processes which lead to youth homelessness, have a different emphasis and character than those for older men and women (whose homelessness may occur at a time of a relationship breakdown).

Data limitations

It is arguable that, in research on homelessness, an explicit recognition of the interdependence between research, policies and service development is essential. Research on homelessness is inherently policy oriented. As with all policy oriented research, homelessness research requires empirical evidence and is (unless it commissions its own surveys) therefore dependent on the quality and integrity of the available data.

Previous publications by FEANTSA (1995) have indicated that primary research targeted on homelessness is rare at the national level and non-existent at the European level[1]. Therefore, estimates of the prevalence of housing exclusion and identification of needs of the homeless population frequently have to be based on data gathered for the purpose of administration of services; such information tends to be partial and frequently incompatible. In these circumstances it was recognised that in drawing up their research reports for this study, the national correspondents of the Observatory had neither the possibility to undertake primary research on a nationally representative sample nor much choice in the selection of available data sources. The problems for cross-national research caused by the absence of comprehensive national data sources is compounded by the lack of compatibility between nations of such data that is collected.

Drawing on the overview of primary data sources collated by Avramov (1996b), it can be seen that EU countries fall into five groups, which range from no reliable primary data sources to a comprehensive national survey on homelessness that pools information from multiple sources. The five groups are summarised below.

In *Greece and Portugal* there are no primary sources which are representative for the country as a whole or for administrative regions or large cities. Shelters for homeless people are the only source of empirical information in *Belgium and Spain*. In the *United Kingdom* only partial data from the public administration of people accepted onto waiting lists for housing (as priority groups) are available for the country as a whole. In *Ireland* administrative data is available for the country as a whole and every two (now three) years local authorities provide estimates of the number of homeless people. In *Austria, Germany, France, Italy and Luxembourg* targeted surveys are the principle source of empirical data, although the aims and methods used in these surveys are radically different. It is only in *Denmark, Finland and Holland* that two or more representative sources can be used to estimate the prevalence of homelessness and to describe the characteristics of homeless people. Even where data is extensively collected (for example, in *Sweden*), diversity in the type and range of data gathered limits transnational comparative analysis.

It is also clear that, in all countries, homeless people who remain outside the institutional framework of emergency services are hidden from official statistics. This will mean that assessments of the level of unmet housing needs and needs for support and care are weak unless complemented by other sources.

Structure of the report

The report begins with two 'context' chapters. Chapter 2 establishes the principles of comparative housing research employed in this study, examines the changing social context in which innovative services are emerging and considers the nature of innovation as it applies to services for the homeless. Chapter 3 focuses explicitly on homelessness, reflecting on the processes which have led to increases in the levels of homelessness and changes in the composition of the homeless population in Europe; the differential manifestation of homelessness in member countries is also considered. Calling on evidence from the national reports of the Observatory's corespondents (see Appendix for case study details), changing views on the nature and causes of homelessness are identified and, in the final section of Chapter 3, we examine the national policy frameworks in which services to the homeless have been devised.

In Chapter 4 the nature and dimensions of innovation in relation to service provision for the homeless are explicitly considered. Following a brief historical overview, attention focuses on the nature of recent innovation; from this we develop a 'a matrix of innovations' which is used as the framework of analysis in the following chapters. The study then moves on to dissect the national case studies, scrutinising them in terms of their innovative contribution on three dimensions: strategic innovation (Chapter 5), organisational innovation (Chapter 6) and operational innovation (Chapter 7). In Chapter 8 we draw out some conclusions with regard to European trends and future research and in the Appendix we present summary details of the case studies drawn from the national reports of the 15 correspondents.

Note

[1] For example, the EUROHOME project on Emergency and Transitory Housing for homeless people. A selection of papers from this project were publicised under the FEANTSA imprint in 1996.

TWO

Welfare, housing and social exclusion: a contextual framework

In this chapter we consider three issues: the nature of comparative housing research; the changing social context in which innovative services for the homeless are emerging in Europe; and the nature of innovation as it relates to services for the homeless.

In this transnational report we opt for a comparative approach that attempts to draw out the similarities between nations and regions in terms of service initiatives for homeless people, while maintaining an awareness of and sensitivity to the specificity of each national and regional situation. In a recent article, Kemeny and Lowe (1998) have labelled this the 'divergent approach', an approach which has been specifically adopted by a number of researchers in their studies of European social policy (Esping-Andersen, 1990; C. Cousins, 1998; Silver, 1997; Daly, 1999). These authors have produced classifications or typologies of European approaches (known as regimes) to welfare, housing and social exclusion. To the extent that such regimes capture similarities and differences between countries in terms of welfare and housing, it is likely that change and innovation in services to the homeless will reflect both the established modes of operation characteristic of each regime (endogenous change) and the responses of each regime to pressures for change emanating from the wider social and economic context of European society (exogenous change). In the context of this study it is exogenously generated innovations that are of particular interest. Over the past two decades, especially, the viability of all European welfare and housing systems has been tested and challenged by pressure from unprecedented processes of economic and social transformation. Overwhelmed by demand from traditionally serviced groups and faced with new demands, the institutions of welfare and housing service delivery, established for the most part in the years immediately following the end of the Second World War, have been found wanting. This 'crisis of the welfare state' has created the conditions (and the opportunity) for radical change and innovation in the way in which welfare and housing services – including those for the homeless – are conceived and delivered. In concluding this chapter, we consider the meaning and nature of innovation in service delivery as it applies to the housing context and to the study of homelessness. In particular, we examine the way structure and agency interrelate to engender institutional change and innovation.

Comparative analysis of housing in the European Union

In their recent review, Kemeny and Lowe (1998) draw a distinction between juxtapositional, convergent and divergent (middle way) approaches to the comparative study of housing. Chronological in their emergence, juxtapositional analysis emphasises the particularities of individual situations comparing nation with nation in terms of observed differences and similarities, while convergent approaches call upon universal and global processes of change to account for the perceived drawing together of policies and trends (unilinear tendencies). The level of explanatory analysis offered by juxtapositional approaches is minimal. In contrast, convergent approaches offer a high level of explanation, but in the process tend to elide and ignore the nuances of the very real differences that exist between nations, regions and localities. Divergent approaches – or "theories of the middle way" (Kemeny and Lowe, 1998, p 170) – arise principally from dissatisfaction with the over-determined nature of convergence theories. As an example of a divergent approach, Kemeny and Lowe cite Esping-Andersen's seminal work (1990) on the identification of a typology of European welfare state regimes. By seeking to produce typologies of welfare, Kemeny and Lowe argue, a divergent approach not only transcends the over-generalisation tendencies of convergence, but also avoids the retreat to the particularism characteristic of the juxtapositional approach.

In our study we attempt to apply a divergent approach in seeking an understanding of the nature and characteristics of homelessness initiatives across Europe[1]. This approach recognises that while each country and region may have its own unique historical and cultural characteristics, there are similarities and commonalities between regions and countries in terms of their welfare and housing trends and policies. These commonalities constitute a set or typology of social policy circumstances within each of which change and innovation are likely to share similar characteristics. However, we would also want to emphasise that there is no necessary or straightforward correlation between regime type and homelessness initiatives. Indeed, while it is certainly the case that innovations emerging within countries with similar regimes and with similar economic, social and political conditions are likely to have a degree of commonality, it has also to be recognised that truly innovative initiatives might sever this association, break the mould and cross boundaries[2].

The social context: typologies of welfare and housing regimes

In this study the term social context refers to both the wider economic and social structures of society – particularly to the changing nature of these structures – and to the institutional forms of welfare delivery. We will examine both aspects, but in attempting to get to grips with the nature of social context as it relates to housing policy, we begin with a consideration of the latter – the institutional form of welfare delivery. The delivery of social services (including housing services) is mediated throughout Europe by welfare state institutions. The way these institutions operate and the way they change in response to wider social and economic changes is, as Judith Allen among others has recognised, an "important variable in transmitting the effects of these wider changes" to vulnerable people, such as the homeless, "who are dependent on state welfare institutions to maintain their daily lives" (Allen, 1998, p 39).

Welfare state regimes

> **A regime is understood as a particular constellation of social, political and economic arrangements which tend to nurture a particular welfare system, which in turn supports a particular pattern of stratification, and then feeds back into its stability. (George and Taylor-Gooby, 1996, p 199)**

Esping-Andersen's influential work on welfare regime typology (1990) embraces the principles of divergent analysis and identifies some of the main dimensions of the social contexts in which housing policy has emerged in Europe. Notwithstanding criticism of Esping-Andersen's work (southern, Mediterranean countries get superficial consideration; the typology is based primarily on income maintenance indices and does not take account of several issues such as the commodification of women through the job market or the impact of a colonial heritage), his typology continues to be widely used and cited. It has not been superseded, though it has been supplemented (see, for example, Abrahamson, 1992; Sainsbury, 1992; Barlow and Duncan, 1994; Ferrera, 1996).

In developing his typology, Esping-Andersen uses three principal criteria of differentiation: degree of decommodification, principles of stratification and state–market relations. Based on these criteria, Esping-Andersen identifies three ideal–typical models of welfare provision in Europe.

- The social democratic (*Nordic*) model is based on the vision of society where social, economic and political citizenship is enjoyed by all; social welfare provision is based on principles of universalism, that is, social benefits are extended to all citizens as a matter of right and decommodified; high standards of equality are promoted and the social conditions of employment are designed to support the well-being of society; the state intervenes more than in other regimes.
- The liberal (*Anglo-Saxon*) model is based on a view of society as composed of anatomised individuals; means-tested benefits seek to ensure that each individual has a basic minimum to survive; relationships between individuals and the state are unmediated; a strong work-ethic prevails and the market is encouraged over other forms of organisation.
- The corporatist/conservative (*Continental*) model is based on the notion of society as composed of groups – state and non-state: churches, families, charitable and other voluntary organisations – with defined roles and reciprocal rights and responsibilities; benefits tend to be linked to work performance and are designed not to disturb status differentials; the state reinforces rights attached to class and profession and the church plays a major political and social role.

Esping-Andersen rather neglects the countries of southern Europe, but others (for example, Abrahamson, 1992; Ferrera, 1996), building on his ideas, have suggested that a distinctive fourth, southern welfare regime can be distinguished. This regime bears some resemblance to the continental model in that it is characterised by a strong reliance on civil society (church, family and private charity) in the provision of welfare support, but it differs in that there is a weak or negligible tradition of state involvement.

Kemeny and Lowe (1998) suggest that comparative studies in housing should emulate those of welfare and be progressed through the development of a typology of housing regimes. These authors, however, do not offer a housing regime typology; they content themselves instead with observing that it might be expected that there would be a very close, albeit complex, relationship between dominant welfare state policies and housing policies[3]. The argument is that social housing provision and services for the homeless are part of the operation of the welfare state – they are the near exclusive preserve of the state and voluntary sector. There is an assumption that the shifts and turns in the orientation and composition of European welfare states have had an impact on the nature of housing provision and hence homelessness policy. As Barlow and Duncan (1994) suggest, liberal welfare regimes will tend to provide state housing as a residual tenure for the worst-off in society while offering covert and not so covert support for individual owner-occupation. Corporatist regimes provide wide-ranging support for social housing, but not to the extent that it will upset established status divisions. In social democratic regimes state intervention in the housing market is most extensive; it tends to be tenure neutral and is aimed at ensuring appropriate and adequate housing consumption for all sections of society.

Housing regimes

Mary Daly (1999) has perhaps taken furthest the work of producing a housing regime typology for Europe. Working within a framework similar to that identified by Kemeny and Lowe (1998), Daly attempts to combine welfare regime characteristics (inputs) with the delivery of housing services (outputs). She produces a fourfold classification that marries in many respects with the earlier work of Esping-Andersen. Indeed, if we supplement Esping-Andersen's welfare typology by adding an additional category to explicitly accommodate the southern European countries, the parallel is complete. In their 1996 analysis of the success and failure of housing provision in Europe, Barlow and Duncan (1994, p 31) suggest that this additional category might be labelled 'the rudimentary welfare type', which they apply to Greece, Portugal, Spain and southern Italy – societies in which there is no right to welfare and support for the needy is provided by family and the church. For our purposes, the relatively unfinished and uncertain form of the welfare state regime emerging in these countries may be better captured in the term 'formative welfare state' (Figure 2.1).

Figure 2.1: European welfare and housing typologies

From Esping-Andersen	From Daly
Social democratic	Scandinavian
Conservative–corporatist	Continental
Liberal	Atlantic**
Formative*	Mediterranean

Notes

* This category is missing from Esping-Andersen's work.

** Daly's typology labels this 'Liberal'; we prefer Atlantic, to maintain the geographic symbolism of the labels.

There are problems and limitations in using such a housing regime typology, as Daly recognises: it can be overly crude and generalising, tending to ignore nuances of difference *within* countries – regional variations, urban/rural and core/periphery contrasts – and it does not take account of the potential impact of decentralised responsibilities, whereby even neighbouring local authorities or regional governments could determine different approaches and hence create the climate for the emergence of different types of innovation. These are scale and governance issues (see Chapter 3). In the context of our study, we need to heed Daly's caveat that, in the same way that we cannot 'read off' housing policy from welfare regimes, there is no easy association or correlation between housing regimes and homelessness policy. She argues that her housing typology should be seen as an heuristic device. The usefulness of the housing typology lies in its attempt to combine both inputs – welfare polices and philosophies – with outputs – social housing provision and levels of homelessness (see also Avramov, 1995.) In identifying nations with similar histories and similar traditions, Daly's typology suggests a grouping of countries in which change and innovation are responding to similar circumstances. For example, in Scandinavian countries – low levels of homelessness, high levels of housing and income support, accessed as a right of citizenship and residence; in Mediterranean countries – low levels of homelessness (based on registered figures), low levels of income maintenance and little tradition of state provision of social housing. The implication here is that we can expect housing policies and hence innovative services for the homeless to be more similar *within* regime type than *between* types.

The changing social context

Change and innovation are inherent in the operation of any non–dormant system; endogenously generated change, however, though non-trivial, is likely to be small in scale, iterative and reinforcing of the existing system. Endogenous changes and innovations in housing and welfare policy, including service delivery to the homeless, have been apparent throughout the post-war period in all countries of the EU. Typically these have taken the form of adjustments to perceived lacuna or gaps in policy and have sought to make service delivery more effective and efficient. As part of the evolution of welfare and housing policies such changes and adjustments reflect the gradual abandonment in the post-war period of a 'medical' model of welfare in favour of a 'social' model; a change which has seen, among other things, a shift from a focus on palliative and curative measures to those which place more emphasis on prevention.

Through the 1980s, in particular, the pace and depth of such changes have been more fundamental and far-reaching, reflecting a heightened sense of the challenge emanating from societal forces exogenous to welfare and housing systems. The linking of the endogenous evolutionary tendencies of welfare systems with more revolutionary changes provoked by exogenous forces has provided the context for major changes in the orientation of welfare and social policy.

Donzelot (1991) summarises these changes when he refers to a movement from 'welfare assistance' and 'welfare protection' to what he terms 'welfare of the third type' (quoted in Tosi, 1997b, pp 92-3). While more conspicuous in those countries where a welfare state has an established history, they are also apparent in countries with formative welfare regimes. In Donzelot's account, welfare assistance, an inheritance from pre-war decades, was provided principally for the control and containment of a *marginalised* population; a population whose condition of pathological dependency was seen as the result of personal inadequacies. Welfare protection marked a progression towards the recognition of the rights of a *normal* population to welfare entitlements; it recognised a need to compensate for basic structural weaknesses in a society that was unable to provide work and appropriate housing for all its members. In the term 'welfare of the third type', which for our purposes can perhaps be more appropriately relabelled 'participatory welfare', Donzelot identifies a further recent shift in welfare policy towards a position where welfare assistance is predicated on the recognition and assumption of responsibilities by recipients to tackle their condition of exclusion and dependency – the recent 'New Deal', workfare programme introduced in Britain is symptomatic of such a development.

Advances in the identification of the causes of welfare problems *and* an improved appreciation and comprehension of how welfare itself can be more efficiently and efficaciously delivered, are very much part and parcel of the 'normal' operation of welfare systems; they are, using our terminology, an endogenous feature of these systems. Yet, as exogenous forces threaten the operation and very survival of these systems, so the development of novel conceptual and theoretical insights becomes critical. Additionally, such 'new times' (Hall and Jacques, 1989) provide the occasion when some hitherto quiescent and neglected issues come to the fore, providing a further possible stimulus for change and innovation (see Neale, 1997 and Pinch, 1997).

In the following section we argue that *fin de siècle* Europe has seen the emergence of exogenous forces in the form of critical economic and social transformations that have tested and challenged the ability of welfare state and housing regimes in the fulfilment of their historic roles. This has created the need, and the opportunity, for change and innovation in the way welfare and housing institutions operate.

Welfare state 'crisis'

The countries of the EU have undergone transformative economic, social and political changes over the past 20 years that were clearly manifest in the 1970s' and 1980s' 'crisis of the welfare state' and in the 'post-crisis' period of adjustment in the 1990s (Mishra, 1990). As a consequence of these changes, welfare states are now struggling not only to adequately service traditional target populations but also, crucially, finding it difficult to respond appropriately to new demands unforeseen when they were originally constructed in the early post-war years. The crisis and transformation of the welfare states in Europe has been linked principally with two main sets of exogenous forces for change: economic restructuring and sociodemographic transformations.

Economic restructuring in Europe, particularly in the industrialised countries of the North and West, in the last quarter of the 20th century, reflects the impact of the latest phase of globalisation. These changes are sometimes characterised as the move from a 'Fordist' to a 'post-Fordist' regime of accumulation. Contentious though these terms are, they have the benefit of encapsulating and identifying largely undisputed changes apparent in the economies of many European nations:

deindustrialisation and rise of a service economy; technological change associated with automation and computerisation; unprecedented (since the 1930s) and sustained high levels of unemployment and, for small but significant sections of society, increasing levels of long-term unemployment; a declining tax base that has had a major impact on public expenditure; a process of social polarisation resulting from increased inequalities, in particular a growing gap between the very rich and the very poor.

Sociodemographic transformations have been evident throughout Europe in such features as: declining fertility; ageing population (itself a tribute to the successes of welfare); increased incidence of divorce; later marriages; larger numbers of childless couples; increased cohabitation; increases in one-parent families; increasing rate of household formation; increasing proportion of women at work; disappearance of the 'traditional' family based on a male breadwinner; and increased levels of migration and of refugees.

The overall effect of these economic and sociodemographic changes has been the creation of a fragmented labour force and social polarisation. Recent policy and theoretical debates have used the concept of 'social exclusion' to encapsulate the impact of these changes. While the impact of economic restructuring and social and demographic transformation has varied between countries, reflecting their different histories and cultures, all countries have experienced social exclusion to a greater or lesser extent, whereby sections of society are not only excluded from and denied access to labour and housing markets but also from full participation in 'society' implicit in citizenship status.

The impact of these economic and social changes on welfare service delivery and social policy (including housing) has resulted in: underfunding and under-resourcing (demands outstrip tax base capabilities) of welfare and social policy; increased demands especially through unprecedented post-war levels of unemployment (but also through increased expectations related in part to technological change, for example, in medicine); new demands on welfare support – introduced by demographic and social changes (for example, one-parent families) and by the increasing incidence of polarisation (increased income inequalities); and the emergence of what appear to be permanent problems of 'social exclusion'.

Coincident with and related to the crisis of the welfare state, there is the suggestion that the political consensus that sustained welfare systems over the past four decades is now eroding. The trans-class alliances that accompanied the initiation of welfare states and supported their development and extension for most of the post-war years have been undermined by the crisis[4]. This erosion creates a climate in which changes and innovations which 'violate' some of the founding principles of provision are more likely to be seen as permissible and legitimate (for example, greater reliance on employment pensions, private insurance and private delivery of care).

The emergence of social exclusion among European populations is a material manifestation of the crisis of the welfare state, indicative of the inability of existing welfare policies to deal with this quintessential welfare phenomenon. Post-war welfare states were formed in a period of traditional families (male breadwinner, women carers at home), low unemployment and lower life expectancy. Such welfare systems were unprepared for the burgeoning demands from traditional target groups and were not designed for, and have proved incapable of coping with or adapting to, the new demands thrown up by economic and social change. The structural and organisational inadequacies of welfare regimes have been exacerbated by a crisis of public funding that casts doubt on the ability and, perhaps, willingness of governments to deliver quality welfare provision. The multi-dimensional problems associated with social exclusion lie outside the normal range of traditional welfare policy, in addition to which the ability of welfare states to adjust and accommodate is thwarted by a lack of resources.

Housing and social exclusion

The concept of social exclusion emerged first in France in 1974 (parallel concepts of 'new poverty' and 'underclass' emerge in Britain and the USA respectively at about the same time) and has subsequently (1989) been embraced by the EU as a European problem worthy of special consideration and resource allocation; in 1990 the 'European Observatory on National Policies for Combating Social Exclusion' was set up. The term social exclusion is variously interpreted and its manifestation varies across the nations and societies that comprise the EU (see Room, 1995). In the broadest, multi-dimensional use of the term, reference is made to three forms of exclusion. The first reference is to exclusion from the economic realm, from employment. This is often regarded as the most crucial since it means lack of access to resources – it means poverty. Second, exclusion from the political process that implies not only lack of political representation and access to decision making, but also lack of power and control over even some of the most elementary of daily activities. Third, exclusion from the cultural arena (because of poverty, race, language and/or lack of education etc) means "marginalisation from [the] symbols, meanings, ritual and discourses" of mainstream society (Madanipour, 1998, p 76).

In considering these issues, Silver (1994) and Christine Cousins (1998) recognise that, while similarities exist between countries in the way social exclusion is manifest, there are subtle and not so subtle variations between nations. To capture these variations they identify a fourfold social exclusion paradigm in which various aspects of social exclusion are emphasised and others play only a minor role. The four paradigms are: solidarity, specialist, monopoly and 'neo-organic'. In the solidarity paradigm, the concept of citizenship is emphasised; it includes political rights and duties and an obligation on the part of the state to aid the inclusion of the excluded. The specialisation paradigm, on the other hand, is underpinned by Anglo-American liberalism, in which social exclusion is seen to reflect discrimination against individuals, market failures and unenforced rights. The monopoly paradigm sees exclusion and poverty as a consequence of the formation of group monopolies. The concept of exclusion here focuses on the notions of social closure, social class and subordination. Christine Cousins develops the fourth 'neo-organic' paradigm from Silver's 'organic' form of social exclusion. It lacks the careful articulation of the other three, but is distinguished by "the pursuit of a social order based on groups, which may be vertical, functional or primordial, that is regional, religious, ethnic or linguistic groups" (C. Cousins, 1998, p 130). Exclusion occurs because some of the groups that comprise civil society are privileged over others; a privileged position that may be reinforced by state intervention. The 'neo-organic' paradigm is also characterised by exclusion based on membership of the core sectors of the labour market that secures access to social assistance; for others there are only weak or no benefits.

Silver and Cousins argue that these paradigms provide a schema both for understanding how social exclusion is differently manifest in the countries of the EU and an explanation of variable policy responses. While Silver wants to resist attribution, on a one-to-one basis, of these paradigms to particular countries, Cousins is happy to point out their correspondence with the welfare regime typology created by Esping-Andersen. By extension we can identify their coincidence with Daly's housing typology.

Figure 2.2: Welfare, housing and social exclusion

Esping-Andersen	Silver	Daly
Social democratic	monopoly	Scandinavian
Conservative–corporatist	solidarity	Continental
Liberal	specialist	Atlantic
Formative	neo-organic	Mediterranean

Both Daly and Silver and Cousins use Esping–Andersen as their reference point in devising their respective schemas. We should not, therefore, be surprised at the close association between the welfare and housing regimes and the social exclusion paradigms identified in Figure 2.2. The social democratic welfare state regime, identified in Esping–Andersen's typology, is characterised by a commitment to full employment and the provision of universal social benefits. This extends, in Daly's typology, to state support for tenure–neutral housing provision designed to counter the monopoly forms of social exclusion based on group elitism identified by Silver and Cousins. The archetypal country is Sweden, with Finland and Denmark also strongly demonstrating these characteristics. The corporatist/conservative welfare regime is status based. Decommodified benefits are universally available to ensure the participation of all within the economic and moral order of society. These welfare regime characteristics marry with a housing regime that provides wide-ranging support for social housing, but not to the extent that it will upset established status divisions; securing a status position in society (including appropriate housing) implies solidarity and guarantees social inclusion. France fits most closely this ideal–typical type; and it can be extended to Austria, Luxembourg, Belgium and (perhaps) the Netherlands. Germany is a more problematic case since, in Christine Cousins' account, on the social exclusion dimension, some of Germany's social characteristics overlap with the 'neo-organic' paradigm. The liberal welfare regime has been most closely associated with the UK and Ireland (but see M. Cousins, 1998). Its social welfare programmes are designed to combat forms of social exclusion occurring as a consequence of market failure ('specialist' in Silver and Christine Cousins' terminology). They are minimally designed to combat only the worst effects of poverty. The contribution of social housing, as an integral part of these programmes, is to provide residual housing for the worst-off in society[5]. The 'neo-organic' paradigm is linked with the formative, Mediterranean societies of Spain, Italy, Greece and Portugal. This welfare regime, based on traditional civil society composed of family, private charity and church organisations politically and ideologically backed by the state, coincides with the provision of housing predominantly from similar private and charitable sources. Failure to secure membership of these traditional civil society groups results in social exclusion.

The failure of the respective welfare and housing regimes, subject to intense external economic and sociodemographic pressures, to effectively deliver social services creates problems of social exclusion. Lack of appropriate housing stands as a clear manifestation of exclusion with homelessness, in particular, being a highly visible indicator. A recent FEANTSA policy report identifies homelessness as "the most extreme manifestation of social exclusion" (FEANTSA, 1999, p 11) in that it combines social dislocation with marginalisation. Social exclusion draws housing into the debate about welfare crisis, linking it in a complex of ways to issues of long-term unemployment and citizenship.

Innovation in services for homeless people

Homelessness, as an integral feature of social exclusion, is a European-wide phenomenon. With social exclusion, there has emerged a European-wide recognition that homelessness is a complex and multi-faceted problem requiring programmes geared to individual needs for successful reintegration. There is also a European-wide recognition that a response to these problems through an expansion of traditional state-based welfare and housing services is, on the one hand, untenable and, on the other, undesirable. The need for fiscal stringency, reflected in a commitment to a reduction in public expenditure in all the countries of the EU, makes expansion untenable; such stringency warrants a contraction rather than expansion of state-delivered services. The inherited institutionalised forms of state-provided services to the homeless make them undesirable as an effective response to homelessness when seen as a facet of social exclusion. This is because many state services (though not all) still demonstrate an institutional commitment to control and containment, to discipline and punishment, as a consequence of which they offer transitory and emergency solutions to homelessness, rather than a commitment to long-term solutions required by a social exclusion perspective[6].

The restructuring of welfare and social systems that have taken place throughout the EU in response to an emergent understanding of homelessness as a facet of social exclusion, indicate a certain commonality of response. Most prominent has been the retreat of the state from the direct provision of welfare services (for reasons cited above) and the assumption of an enabling and regulatory role. No less prominent – and paralleling the changing role of the state – has been the re-emergence of voluntary agencies (non-governmental agencies [NGOs]) as alternative providers of welfare and related services to the homeless. In those countries characterised by formative welfare regimes (that is, where the state's welfare role was always limited), the enhanced role of voluntary agencies has been no less marked, responding to new and increasing demands. New, innovative forms of service provision have emerged and these vary between regimes types, but they cannot be read off in any mechanistic way on the basis of regime characteristics; innovation and change reflect *not only* the inherited traditions, customs and bureaucratic arrangements of the different regimes, *but also* the action of conscious agents acting in the context of permissive and constraining structural conditions. An investigation of innovation and change in service provision to the homeless needs to recognise the interactive roles both of inherited structures and of proactive agents; an interaction that can be complex and sometimes unpredictable.

Innovation: structure and agency

Social science, in seeking to understand the changing nature of society and of human behaviour, has skipped between deterministic (structural) and voluntaristic (agency) modes of explanation. Recognised as a false dichotomy, the search for a tenable middle ground between these two extremes has dominated social science thinking for more than two decades. Perhaps Anthony Giddens (1979, 1984) has come closest to providing a resolution to this 'agency-structure debate'. Giddens' structuration theory sees agents and structures as symbiotically interrelated, neither exists without the other. Structures created by human agency can be changed by human agency; they are malleable and susceptible to change. But in seeking to change and innovate at whatever scale – macro, meso or micro – pre-existing structures (traditions, rules, bureaucratic and institutional forms etc) can prove to be constraining as well as permissive. In Giddens' phraseology this interrelationship between structures, given and inherited from the past, and active agents, is identified as the process of *structuring*.

Who are the structuring agents in the context of innovative services to the homeless? The main agents of change and innovation in relation to the delivery of services to the homeless have traditionally been identified as: social workers and agencies as well as, more recently, housing policy makers and funders, housing managers and housing workers, working respectively at strategic (coordination and national/regional policy initiatives), organisational (defining targets and new project initiatives) and operational (service delivery, user involvement) levels. The roles of these agents and their respective levels of operation are elaborated in Chapter 4. Agents working at these levels have the opportunity and responsibility to innovate in response to increased and new demands placed on housing service systems, and in response to diminishing and finite resources. The best of these innovations take on board the notion of homelessness as a facet of social exclusion. Judgement of an innovation then would take into account not only its success in providing shelter, but also the extent to which, by assisting in the development of social networks (occupational, political and cultural), it had an impact on the everyday lives of homeless people in allowing them to cohere and integrate with mainstream society or some identifiable and supportive community.

The traditional roles of these structuring agents of housing policy and provision have now to be complemented by the advent of what has become known as 'user involvement'; the users of services emerging as agents in their own right in determining the type of services offered and the conditions under which they are provided. This development links to the development of a 'third type' of welfare delivery (see Donzelot, 1991, cited earlier), to the development of what we have labelled 'participatory welfare'.

The emergence of participatory welfare has been stimulated by two conflicting tendencies. First, an ideology of individualism that requires acceptance of 'responsibility' in return for access to services and, second, debates over the nature of control and discipline. The two are conflicting because the former is based on the drawing up of a contract – imposed and rarely negotiated – between homeless individuals and service providers. Through this contract the homeless become responsible for their own 'normalisation', their integration into mainstream society; they conform by learning the disciplines of time management and financial prudence and the principles of acceptable interpersonal and social behaviour. The latter, in contrast, is based on a view of societal structures and processes as power structures and processes, oppressing and 'colonising' individuals (see Foucault, 1979). Thus homeless people's lives are colonised in the sense that, as a condition of service provision, they are 'forced' into conformity and compliance with the norms of the wider society. Foucault's complex view of power and power relations embraces the notion of 'resistance' on the part of the individuals and

23

groups involved. Participatory welfare for homeless people, in the sense that it implies user involvement in the design and operation of services, creates the conditions for 'resistance' in which the notions of normalisation and reintegration can, potentially, be challenged and reformulated.

Conclusion

The central argument of this chapter has been that exogenous change provides a catalyst for rethinking and reformulation. Sociodemographic and economic transformations have created the conditions for innovation and change and offered a challenge to the way in which welfare and housing services – including services to the homeless – have traditionally been delivered. Our analytical framework suggests that the manner of response will be determined by a complex interaction of structural constraints – inherited systems of delivery and fiscal stringency – and active agency on the part of policy makers, housing workers and, perhaps increasingly, users of the services. These responses have demonstrated some commonalities across all EU countries; the contraction of state-provided services and the concomitant expansion of NGO activity, for example. But other responses, as the case studies of this report demonstrate, are specific to particular countries and regions. The extent to which innovations developed in one set of circumstances can be effectively transferred to other circumstances is an issue for consideration in the concluding chapter of this report.

Notes

[1] A regime approach has its critics (for example, Harloe, 1995) and its supporters (for example, Kleinman, 1996).

[2] Such a process may be more likely in the context of growing unification of Europe. Closer alliance reflects growing familiarity, the sharing of ideas across national and regional boundaries.

[3] There is no direct relationship because, unlike other elements of welfare – education, health, income maintenance – housing provision has not been decommodified (the market has never been fully replaced) even in social democratic regimes. See also Kemeny (1995).

[4] It is possible to overestimate this effect (see Esping-Andersen, 1990) and difficult to marry with the notion of rising expectations.

[5] Social housing stock – such that is left – is associated with an earlier phase when social democratic imperatives were more prominent.

[6] See, however, Kleinman (1996) who argues that bifurcation is the predominant characteristic.

THREE

Context of service provision

This chapter aims to describe the historic and present day context within which the provision of services for homeless people may be examined. First, processes common to all countries in the EU, which have resulted in increased levels of homelessness and insecure and/or inadequate housing for low–income groups, are identified. Second, national trends in individual countries in levels of homelessness and in the provision for the homeless are outlined, and finally, the changing views of homelessness, in different national contexts, are considered and common threads distinguished.

Processes of change

A number of developments, some of which were touched upon in Chapter 2, may be identified across Europe which result in increased levels of homelessness and insecure, inadequate housing for low-income groups. These changes are briefly discussed below.

Demographic changes have meant that more people are living alone as single adults for longer periods than in previous decades. Couples are less stable, and are more likely to get separated. As life expectancy has been extended, more people are living independently for longer periods after retirement. The combination of these demographic changes means that the rate of new household formation is in many countries much higher than the rate of net population growth. The result is that the level of demand for housing units, and in particular for those that are suitable for smaller households, has grown rapidly.

Socioeconomic changes have resulted from major trends such as economic globalisation, market liberalisation, industrial restructuring and technological advances, which have all combined to bring about big reductions in the numbers of well-paid stable full-time jobs in some, especially the traditional, economic sectors. Thousands of redundant workers have been forced either to depend on restricted social welfare benefits, or to take insecure low-paid jobs. Growing numbers of people are to be found living in poverty, on low or sometimes no income at all. Most of these people simply cannot afford to pay for adequate accommodation on the private housing market and many are even denied access to the social housing market.

Changes in social welfare provision have impacted on an increasing number of people. As the numbers of unemployed and low-paid workers have grown, so more individuals and families have been left with no choice but to depend on payments and services made available through systems of social welfare. The situation varies widely between different countries but there has been a general trend towards limiting the levels of social welfare benefits, which in many cases have fallen in relation to average incomes, while imposing tighter restrictions on their availability, in terms of tough conditions that people must meet before they can receive payments. In most countries, young people up to 25 years of age now have fewer rights than those over 25 in terms of gaining access to welfare benefits, and especially to payments allocated to cover housing costs. Meanwhile, concerning the most vulnerable adults – those with mental illness, or drug and alcohol related problems – there has been a shift away from institutional care towards community-based services. However, the resources allocated to these services are often not sufficient for a proper response to the specific needs of individual cases.

Changes in the housing market have affected an increasing number of households as a result of the privatisation of housing, decentralisation of responsibilities and the changing roles of voluntary sector housing agencies such as housing associations. There has been a general decline in the provision of social rented housing in the public sector, by local authorities or by non-profit associations, as governments have reduced levels of public investment. In some countries (such as the UK and Italy) there has been a significant reduction in the supply of social housing as a result of its sale to the occupants or to private landlords. The current housing tenure structure of member states is shown in Table 3.1. Meanwhile, the deregulation of the private rental sector has led to increases in rent levels. This trend towards substitution of the public rental sector by private rental housing, ruled by the laws of the market, has led to low-income groups becoming increasingly dependent on housing benefit payments (where these are available). This is coupled with the move away from capital investment in housing stock towards restricted funding of individual benefits within the social welfare budgets: the availability of housing benefit payments has been curtailed in most countries as pressures on the public budget have increased.

Table 3.1: Housing tenure in the European Union (1995) (%)

	Owner-occupation	Privately rented	Social housing	Other tenures
Austria	41	22	23	14
Belgium	62	30	7	-
Denmark	50	24	18	8
Finland	72	11	14	3
France	54	21	17	8
Germany	38	36	26	-
Greece	70	26	-	4
Ireland	80	9	11	-
Italy	67	8	6	19
Luxembourg	67	31	2	-
Netherlands	47	17	36	-
Portugal	65	28	4	3
Spain	76	16	2	-
Sweden	43	16	22	19
United Kingdom	66	10	24	-
EU average	56	21	18	5

Source: After Balchin (1996, Table 1.12, p 11)

National and regional trends

Chapter 1 referred to the general picture of homelessness in the 15 EU countries where, it is estimated, approximately 3 million people have no fixed home of their own (FEANTSA, 1995). While the evidence indicates some amelioration in the growth of homelessness in some countries in recent years, the most significant characteristic of homelessness across the EU during the last 30 years has been its persistence and resistance to previous policy responses.

Changes in social welfare systems, constraints on public sector spending, the privatisation of public sector social housing, the increase in unemployment and the processes of deinstitutionalisation have all played a role in the growth in homelessness. While these factors can be seen more or less universally in all 15 member states, their extent and impact has been felt differently both between states and even within member states on a regional basis. In addition to these factors, migration to urban areas and in-migration of immigrant workers and asylum seekers have contributed to pressures on already extended housing markets.

The following section will highlight the changes in each country for which information is available. For purposes of presentation, countries are grouped together according to the broad housing typology discussed in Chapter 2. Following the divergence model adopted in this report, similarities and differences between countries within each regime will be highlighted in the conclusions to each sub-section.

Broadly speaking, Austria, Belgium, France, Germany, Luxembourg and the Netherlands approach most closely the *Continental* or *conservative– corporatist type* of welfare state and housing regimes.

Austria

In Austria (Kofler, 1998), actual homelessness (people living on the streets) is not a major problem. However, concern is growing over the risks of homelessness to vulnerable and socially excluded people. Increased competition in the labour market and economic restructuring have meant that more people are either unemployed or working in insecure and low-paid positions. Their diminishing incomes cannot meet the costs of housing in a market where the mismatch between supply and demand has increased the costs of rental. Awareness of the threat of homelessness arising from these factors is growing among service providers.

The social rented sector in Austria is roughly the same size as the private rented sector (23% and 22% respectively), and housing subsidies are widely available. Social welfare provision is two-tier, with a universal social security system, which is backed up by the social welfare system where the individual is not eligible for unemployment insurance. Public welfare legislation, passed at the end of the Second World War and still valid today, is inspired by the dual principles of individualisation and subsidiarity.

Within the Austrian context, housing provision and employment are seen as two closely intertwined factors which go hand in hand in preventing homelessness. However, housing and labour policies in general and services in particular continue to work at arm's length from each other. Since the early 1980s, social policies for homeless people have entered a new stage with a trend towards increased differentiation between specialised services and a growing involvement of social services and church-related charity organisations.

Belgium

The rise in homelessness in Belgium (de Decker, 1998) can be attributed to a number of factors. First, the economic restructuring which started to impact in the 1980s has led to significant changes in the labour market. These changes can be characterised by the rise in unemployment and the fall in employment security leading to a polarisation of socioeconomic groups.

Second, the hegemony of home ownership in Belgian housing policy (62% of all housing stock in 1995) has led to very limited investment in and development of the social housing sector (7% of total housing stock in 1995). The private rental sector is the second most important segment of the housing market despite its declining share. The legislation governing the private rental sector is based on the Civil Code and inspired by a conservative philosophy which promotes the interests of landlords. The only structural alternative for housing in Belgium is through home ownership but, because of the high costs, this option is not readily available to low-income groups and is wholly inaccessible to those who are socially excluded.

Third, demographic changes which are manifest in the growth in the number of new households being formed, despite a stagnation in the birth rate, has increased demand for new smaller and affordable housing units. Average household size in Belgium has decreased from 3 in 1970 to 2.5 in 1991. The characteristics of single-person households have also changed, with a growing shift from the typical single elderly person living in widowhood to younger unmarried or divorced people. Single-income households generally have less to spend on housing.

This demand for suitable housing for lower-income groups has not been matched by supply. Especially during the economic crisis of the 1980s, the actual levels of construction fell severely and were further exacerbated by the freeing of the private rental market. The extreme housing pressures led to the introduction of 'new products' by private landlords where rooms, and sometimes even mattresses, were let to people who could not afford the market rents for decent housing. At the end of the 1980s, private house building rose again but without reaching its earlier levels. Although the non-profit construction programme was re-launched in Flanders, the level of new build was insufficient to meet demands. In addition, no new social housing programme was introduced in either Brussels Capital region or in Wallonia. Such regional variations and differences might be expected to continue while policies on homelessness and welfare remain the responsibility of individual regions.

Belgian housing policy has generally been broadly directed with, at times, limited exclusion for high-income groups. The historical position has been to give as many people as possible some element of support rather than to provide more substantial support to a more focused target group. The effect of these policies has been to subsidise middle and higher-income groups while the considerably greater needs of lower-income groups have, relatively speaking, been neglected.

France

In France (de Gouy, 1998), homelessness has been increasing since the early 1990s. The increase in unemployment, population growth and the effects of housing policy on construction levels are the main reasons for the growth in the size of the homeless population. In the early 1990s, it is reported that some 200,000 people were homeless, more than 600,000 were living in temporary accommodation or mobile homes, and a further 1.4 million people were living in sub-standard housing.

In the post-war era, an increase in the birth rate in conjunction with immigration has resulted in a 40% growth in population. When this figure is coupled with the substantial level of urbanisation (an estimated 75% of the population now live in cities), we can see that demographic changes have had a sizeable impact on the demand for housing. Certain areas of the country, such as in the north (Tourcoing), have experienced large population growth due to an influx of both French and immigrant workers recruited to work in industrial areas. More recent technological and market changes in these areas have had a significant impact on the size of the unemployed population. These changes, coupled with a shortage of affordable housing and the inaccessibility of employment-related housing for unemployed people, have resulted in an increase in homelessness.

Large-scale social housing construction began later in France than, for example, Germany or the UK, and even today the social housing sector remains smaller than the private rental sector (17% and 21% respectively). The late introduction of the social housing sector and the comparatively large role of the private rental sector, where rent control measures have had a dampening effect on the levels of construction, have affected access to affordable housing. Although local authorities act as enablers and purchasers, the bulk of social housing is provided by the Habitations à Loyer Modérées (HLMs).

French housing policy has historically favoured supporting all sectors of the population. However, the growing costs of this policy were recognised by the late 1970s and a shift from the more indiscriminate bricks and mortar form of subsidy to a more targeted personal housing allowance was introduced. The timing of the shift (1977) coincided with an increase in unemployment and in the proportion of relatively poor or retired people. The end result was a slow down in construction in all tenure types. Thus, just as the demand for affordable housing was increasing, the supply decreased to create a new and widening gap between demand and supply.

A universal right to housing has been enshrined in French legislation but has not been adequately supported by resource incentives for the creation of permanent housing. Instead, the general emphasis of provision in France has been on short-term or emergency housing which does not fully meet the needs of homeless people.

Germany

Until the early 1980s, Germany (Busch-Geertsema, 1998) was able to meet housing demand through a large-scale construction effort which had created a surplus of housing. After this period of relatively good access to housing, Germany began to experience a housing shortage and rise in homelessness in the late 1980s arising from a combination of a growth in the birth rate plus in-flow of immigrants and migrant workers which exerted pressure on the housing market. The rising levels of demand in the late 1980s have been partially but not wholly met by renewed construction. Because of these growing unmet demands, there has been a significant rise in emergency and temporary provision and the re-emergence of many types of provisional accommodation which had not been used in Germany in previous years.

German housing policy is based on an incentive and promotion system which extended to all sectors; it can thus be seen as nearly tenure neutral. More recently, however, there has been a shift to more targeted housing subsidies. It is the German subsidy and loan system which defines the nature of the housing sector rather than the status of the landlord. The social rented sector is thus a fluid sector in which different types of landlords can participate and a sector in which accommodation can move in and out depending on the nature of the subsidy contract and the term of the loan (usually a maximum of 35 years). The size of the social housing sector in West Germany will have halved between 1980 and the year 2000 as a result of the expiry of the time limits on these term loans associated with a majority of the stock which was built in the 1950s and 1960s. Following unification, only about half of the 'social' housing stock of the former German Democratic Republic (GDR) was reserved for people on low incomes (the exact amount depends on Länder laws and local agreements). Rents for this housing stock, owned by municipal housing societies or by *Genossenschaften*, are likely to be relatively high since they are not subject to rent limits and most will require extensive modernisation work.

What characterises the German housing market is the size of its private rental sector which, in 1995, accounted for 36% of all housing stock. This is the largest private rental market of all the member states and its growth can be attributed to the tenure neutral use of housing subsidies and incentives to construct new houses.

The structure of German housing policy is determined by the federal government but its implementation is largely the responsibility of the *Länder* (states) and there is a significant role for the *Gemeinden* (local authorities). The (financial) responsibility laid down in the Federal Welfare Act (and its associated regulations) distinguishes between 'persons without a settled way of life', accommodated in institutions at the cost of state agencies on the Länder level, and other homeless persons who fall under the financial responsibility of the municipalities. Police laws place the responsibility for the provision of temporary accommodation for roofless persons exclusively on municipalities (and not the federal state). However, while many municipalities provide temporary accommodation for families and, sometimes, for those single persons who have been evicted from a local dwelling, other single homeless persons and especially non-local 'vagrants' or 'persons without a settled way of life' are referred to voluntary sector institutions.

Luxembourg

The history of services for vulnerable people in Luxembourg (Pels, 1998) has been dominated by the work of religious organisations and, more recently, the work of secular or secularised voluntary sector organisations. During the 1960s the state, which had traditionally played a very limited role in the development and coordination of such services, was faced with three choices: either a complete take over of social service provision, or no intervention in social service provision and the maintenance of the status quo, or shared responsibility between private (voluntary) and state agencies in the delivery of social services. The state opted for the third model and has since played a significant role as the commissioning/purchasing agent for all social services under the auspices of diverse ministries.

The role adopted by the state has provided voluntary sector organisations with a stable and long-term source of income while, at the same time, safeguarding their freedom of action in the field. The state, as the coordinating body, is to some extent inhibited by the principle of subsidiarity. On the other hand, the system of commissioning and funding does tend to restrict the operational framework of specific projects. Inconsistencies in the requirements of commissioning agents both between and within ministries mean that service providers are constantly striving to meet different demands placed on them. In 1991, a Bill was introduced to regulate relations between the state and agencies working in the social, family and therapeutic domains. However, the Bill has yet to become law.

Luxembourg has the smallest social housing sector of all the member states, accounting for only 2% of the total stock. The remainder of the stock is split in a nearly 2:1 ratio between the owner-occupied sector and the private sector. The ethos of working with the private sector and of embracing the market economy is thus well established.

Netherlands

In the Netherlands (de Feijter, 1998), demographic changes since the Second World War have placed a high demand on housing in a country with the highest population density in the EU. Between 1945 and 1991, the population grew by 61% as a result of both an above-average birth rate and high levels of immigration. In response to this high demand for housing, Dutch housing policy has been characterised by the extensive use of subsidies for new construction and by a focus on planning. Although historically housing subsidies have been aimed at all sectors, the need to contain spending has driven a shift in policy first outlined in the 'Policy Document on Housing in the 1990s'. This shift is characterised by more focused targeting of housing allowances and subsidies to those who are most needy, greater reliance on market and capital finance, as well as a relaxation of rent controls.

The shift in housing policy in the 1990s also included decentralisation of responsibilities, with the local authorities taking greater responsibility for provision of housing, regulation of housing associations and the operation of grant schemes for housing providers. The result has been increased involvement by housing associations and a reliance on market practices. The erosion of the central government role has given way to a diversity of local authority practices with services for the homeless determined by the contractual arrangements between the local authority as enabler/purchaser and a variety of service providers.

Access to affordable housing in good condition in the Netherlands remains a problem. Although social housing is proportionally the largest in the EU (36% of total housing stock), the level of demand for social housing is high. People looking for affordable housing are therefore forced to look to the private rental market, which is more accessible, but of lower quality. Houses in multiple occupation are an important segment of the market and are used by those who cannot afford normal housing. This type of housing may be more accessible for single persons but is much less suitable for families. The difficulties of finding appropriate accommodation for families who may be homeless can be further seen in the overall provision for homeless people, which appears to favour those who are single or those who have special needs.

The availability of cheap housing stock in the Netherlands has been diminished through refurbishment and quality improvements, general rent increases, sales to tenants and demolition. In addition, urban regeneration programmes have resulted in the closure of older, cheaper housing and boarding houses which traditionally accommodated homeless people. In the Netherlands, the tenure neutral approach, associated with all six countries grouped under the Continental/corporatist regime type, has come under sustained pressure during the 1990s.

Demographic changes (particularly in the Netherlands, Germany and France) and growing unemployment in all six states have exerted pressure on public spending and social housing at a time when economic restructuring and changes in housing policy have spurred a slow down in the construction of new homes. The result has been a mismatch between growing housing demand and shrinking housing supply. In certain countries (France, the Netherlands, Austria and, to some extent, Germany), the prevailing policies of tenure neutral housing subsidies are being replaced by more focused spending targeted at poorer people. With the exception of West Germany, the shift away from bricks and mortar subsidies to personal housing allowances has inhibited new construction with the result that the search for affordable housing in good condition is now focused on maximising the use of existing stock, particularly in the private rental sector. In particular in Belgium, France, and Luxembourg, as we shall see in later chapters, innovative initiatives are deliberately focused on the use of existing and often older stock in the private sector to cope with growing demands.

Within some countries, regional variations are evident as the regions determine social welfare and/or housing policy. This is particularly the case in Belgium, Austria and, to a lesser extent, Germany. Yet, even in the more centralised states such as the Netherlands, the move towards decentralisation is set to place greater responsibility on local authorities to coordinate services for homeless people.

Notwithstanding major historical differences (M. Cousins, 1998), Ireland and the UK can be seen within the *Atlantic/Liberal* framework of welfare state and housing regimes. They share the common experiences of the effects of a systematic policy of privatisation and a growing and greater reliance on the unfettered operation of market forces.

Ireland

In Ireland (O'Sullivan, 1998), there is a lack of systematic research on the size and characteristics of the homeless population. Local authorities have a statutory responsibility to count the number of homeless people in their areas every two or three years, but data available are patchy and, in the absence of a clear definition of homelessness, are prone to underestimation. In 1996, half of all local authorities reported no homelessness in their areas. In the remaining 50% of local authorities, 2,501 people were recorded as officially homeless. This is almost certainly an underestimate. Impressionistic data from voluntary organisations who deal with the homeless and the impact of rising levels of unemployment, deinstitutionalisation and numbers of single parents, would indicate that levels are much higher and have been growing through the 1980s.

Prior to 1988, services for the homeless were provided exclusively by charitable (including church) and voluntary organisations. Partly in response to vociferous campaigning by these organisations, the 1988 Housing Act included some reference to homelessness and, for the first time, attributed statutory responsibility for homelessness to local authorities. This legislation enables local authorities to allocate some of their housing stock to homeless people. The local authority can work with approved voluntary agencies in providing accommodation and provide rental and financial assistance to homeless people. Introduced at a time when social housing stock had become residualised (accounting for only 11% of all tenures in 1995 due to the sale of 200,000 council houses to sitting tenants since the mid-1970s), and at a time when local authorities were looking for reductions in public expenditure, take-up of these responsibilities has been poor. The 1991 Child Care Act is the only other piece of legislation that refers to homelessness. It attributes responsibility to health boards for accommodating children up to 18 years.

The strong family traditions and ties that characterise Ireland and the continuing role of the voluntary and church-related organisations disguises the extent and nature of homelessness in Ireland without providing satisfactory solutions for what is becoming a prominent social problem.

United Kingdom

In the United Kingdom (Aldridge, 1998), housing policy has always been tenure specific with lower-income groups being directly targeted. The social housing sector is well developed although, since the 1980s, sales of local authority stock to tenants and transfer programmes to housing associations have significantly reduced the size of stock owned by local authorities. Rent controls and rent regulation have been tighter and lasted longer than elsewhere in Europe, with the notable exception of Spain. Private rental stock, which has been contracting over many years, is the smallest tenure sector in the UK, amounting to 10% of all housing stock.

Central government is responsible for the development of housing policy while local authorities are responsible for its application. With the exception of Northern Ireland and Scotland, where separate legislation is enacted, regional variation is limited to interpretation of legislation and local authorities have no jurisdiction for varying levels of benefits.

The legislative frameworks in the UK have been characterised by the abruptness of some changes in direction and the frequency with which new legislation has been introduced. The change in policy direction introduced in the late 1970s and carried out throughout the 1980s has meant a reduction in house building, a focus on improvement of existing stock and the divestment of public sector housing to individual households (through the tenant's Right to Buy) and housing associations (through large-scale voluntary transfers).

The introduction of the 1977 Homeless Persons Act placed responsibility on local authorities to provide housing for vulnerable people who are unintentionally homeless. Although originally designed to provide permanent housing for homeless people, more recent interpretation of the Act has favoured the provision of short-term accommodation. Families with children and those who are considered vulnerable due to special needs have benefited from the provisions of the legislation. However, people who may be deemed 'intentionally' homeless and single people in general are not covered by the legislation. The 1995 Asylum and Immigration Act specifically excluded asylum seekers, and people on appeal from the 1977 provision, suggesting that the numbers of homeless people awaiting decisions on their asylum status are not currently being counted among the homeless population.

Broadly speaking, Greece, Italy and Spain, in that they share a common reliance on civil society in welfare provision, can be seen within the *Mediterranean framework for welfare state and housing regimes*. Portugal also falls within this model, in our opinion.

Greece

In Greece (Sapounakis, 1998) the visibility and size of the homeless population has grown since the 1980s. Whereas homelessness has been traditionally seen in terms of specific groups who are vulnerable to a breakdown in social relations (principally elderly people and young people), recent demographic and economic changes have contributed to a rise in and diversification of the homeless population. However, there is no reliable data on the size of the problem.

The influx of Greek repatriates from the former Soviet Union and the inflow of migrant workers from Eastern Europe, Albania and the Middle East have exerted pressure on labour and housing markets. At the same time, the loosening of traditional family ties has meant that fewer people are able to rely on the family support network for access to housing. The homeless population in Greece is now recognised to include elderly people, young people, ex-offenders, single women, people suffering from chronic diseases and people with mental illness; in short, people who are largely excluded from the labour market.

Housing policy in Greece does not explicitly recognise the issue of homelessness and there is no official or reliable data on the size of the problem. Social housing provision has traditionally been minimal and accessible only to low-income groups in employment. This system excludes large groups of people who are most vulnerable due to unemployment, disability, and age or erratic patterns of employment. Although some emergency and short-term services for homeless people do exist, these are not linked to any longer-term housing solutions and clients' only option is to find housing on the limited private rental market. The Greek social welfare system is underdeveloped and the family continues to be the principal source of protection for vulnerable groups.

Italy

In Italy (Tosi, 1998), homelessness is seen as a consequence of social exclusion due to direct exposure to risk conditions and against which the existing social welfare system provides inadequate protection. The current social security system, based on an insurance model, favours certain risk situations, usually associated with permanent employment, thereby neglecting a considerable section of the population who are socially excluded. While relatively wide protection is afforded to 'workers' and to categories excluded from the labour market on the basis of factors considered to be 'objective' (for example, old age, disability), unprotected adults are entrusted to a specific welfare assistance system, which as a rule is separate from the main body of social protection policies and is heavily characterised by its discretionary nature and measures largely aimed at emergency situations. All these traits are accentuated when the welfare assistance system deals with social marginalisation. Intervention on behalf of the homeless is positioned in this area. The social welfare system recognises homeless people as its customers only in particular and circumscribed cases. Access to social housing has been traditionally linked to employment insurance policies but even the right to social housing in these circumstances is curtailed by the limited supply of such provision. Social welfare policy is divorced from both housing and employment policies and the separation of the three has led to the residualisation of housing support measures aimed at the marginalised homeless population.

The effects of the insurance model can be seen in the polarisation between, on the one hand, those with permanent employment who can count on a guaranteed system of security should their situation change and, on the other hand, those in temporary, casual or erratic employment with hardly any protection at all. This polarisation is brought into sharp focus when considered within the context of profound restructuring of the labour market. The existing social welfare system in Italy has been traditionally characterised by massive assignment of responsibility for care to families and this is underlined by the fact that 93% of social welfare spending consists of transfers to families. The growing limits of families to supply welfare protection are now pushing the system to its edge.

In the absence of full social rights for the homeless, it is thus inevitable that intervention (reflecting specific traditions of governance and the role of civil society) is distinguished by wide powers of discretion and variability as well as by the prevalence of emergency thinking aimed above all at providing stop-gap measures for the most visible and serious situations.

Portugal

Portugal (Bruto da Costa, 1998) is placed last among the 15 member states in the 1997 EC Report on Poverty. It has been suggested (Freitas, 1998) that, for some time, the main manifestation of poverty in Portugal has been that of families experiencing difficulty competing in the housing market and living in slums or other neighbourhoods without adequate infrastructure. It is estimated that around half a million families in Portugal are in housing need. In order to improve living conditions, the central government can support low-income households by subsidising interest payments when they buy or build a house. Some government support is also given for the construction of social housing, although this is limited by financial constraints. A large resettlement programme was initiated in 1993 as a political response to social and housing problems (Program Especial de Realojament [PER]) and is aimed at improving the housing conditions of families living in shanty settlements (*barracas*). The programme is focused on the metropolitan areas of Lisbon and Oporto. Under this programme the central government will provide a direct subsidy of 40% of the cost of new dwellings and lends another 40% of the cost at very low interest rates. Freitas (1998) argues that the PER reflects both a wide public discussion about the failure of other resettlement experiences and the problems they caused and an ambition to eradicate all slums and *barracas* before the end of the century. In this context the PER is seen as a tool in fighting social exclusion. It should also involve change in the role of different agencies and social actors involved in its implementation, including NGOs and changing perception of the role of the family.

Greece, Spain, Portugal and Italy have traditionally had little or no state intervention in housing or social policy. Until recently, the role of the family and the church in meeting housing needs has been unquestioned. However, demographic and economic pressures have given rise to a more visible homeless population with diverse and complex needs, which can no longer be adequately met by the informal sector. The virtual absence of social housing, coupled with the very limited social welfare systems, has exacerbated problems of access to affordable housing. In all four countries, recognition of the issues of homelessness and the complex needs of homeless people are new and emerging phenomena.

Spain

Spain (Leal Maldonado and Lainez Romano, 1998) has seen a change in the size and composition of the homeless population since the 1970s. The traditional view of the homeless person as a male alcoholic has now given way to greater recognition of the diversity and complexity of needs within the homeless population. Immigration from North Africa and other areas since the mid-1970s, together with rural–urban migration, has placed pressures on Spain's housing markets, especially in the larger urban areas.

There is a virtual absence of social housing stock and owner-occupation is the norm with a small private rental sector. Until recently, Spain has had very strict rent controls in the private sector, which have resulted in the decline of that sector in favour of owner-occupation. The norm in Spain has been to subsidise construction programmes. This subsidy system, which initially targeted developers, has been refocused in favour of individual families and households and, more recently, has been used to rehabilitate and purchase second-hand dwellings. Spain's financial system underwent substantial deregulation in the 1980s, which gave rise to a boom in house prices and resulted in a lack of affordable housing.

Since the 1970s, housing policy has been devolved to 17 Autonomous Communities or Regions. However, this has had very little effect on housing policy since the Autonomous Communities have no housing stock which they manage or over which they have influence. The

Autonomous Communities' principal role in relation to housing is the distribution of the personal aid system according to rules laid down by the central government. However, the Autonomous Communities also have the ability to supplement such schemes from their own funds.

Denmark, Finland and Sweden can be seen as most closely approximating the *Nordic/social democratic model of welfare state and housing regimes.*

Denmark

Data from Denmark (Børner Stax, 1998) in the 1980s and 1990s show an increase in the number of people using services for homeless people. Although this data suggest an increase in the homeless population, it may also be a feature of the recording and registration system since smaller institutions, previously excluded, are now included in the official count. The speed with which deinstitutionalisation of the psychiatric sector is being implemented is not necessarily matched by the speed of alternative provision for people leaving large-scale institutional care. The mismatch between demand and supply for people with special needs may exacerbate the homelessness problem.

Paragraph 105 of the 1976 Social Assistance Act identifies the responsibilities of regional counties and the municipalities of Copenhagen and Frederiksberg for the homeless. Initially, this responsibility merely required the provision of temporary shelter. Recent legislative changes, however, have extended this remit in two ways. First, the responsibilities of the regional counties and municipalities have been extended to include the development of reintegration programmes for people who reside in Section 105 institutions for a minimum of three months and, second, the responsibilities of the Section 105 institutions have been extended to those at risk of homelessness (for example, drug users and the mentally ill) as well as those who are without shelter. The reintegration programmes have several dimensions: the provision of a contact/support worker for homeless individuals from outside the Section 105 institutions and the establishment of shared dwellings as both an alternative to Section 105 institutions for permanent residence and as a transitional form of residence prior to full integration. In addition, direct movement to individually tenanted flats is also favoured for suitable individuals. In securing alternative accommodation the municipalities have nomination rights with non-profit housing organisations as well as, on a more limited basis, with the private sector.

Finland

Data in Finland (Kärkkäinen and Hassi, 1998) shows that, as a result of policy programs since the mid-1980s, the numbers of 'houseless' people has decreased between 1987 and 1996 (18,000 and 10,000 respectively). However, provision for those who are homeless is no less difficult to access and there is a waning of government (both central and local) interest in catering for the needs of homeless people. In fact, the housing focus is on mainstream and supported housing with emergency provision closing down.

Finland operates a system of universal provision for basic social security, social and health services irrespective of working careers. Its benefit system is financed through employer and employee taxation collected by both central and municipal government with private insurance schemes playing a modest role. Until recently, the 1990s have been a period of economic recession marked by high unemployment (13%). In part, this has resulted in an erosion of rationally devised political objectives in social policy in favour of fragmentary, community-based policies where the issues of homelessness, the activation of marginalised people and self-governance are taking shape.

The Finnish system of government includes 455 municipalities which, like the Swedish, have considerable autonomy, including the right to levy taxes. Responsibility for the planning and implementation of housing, social welfare policy and service provision lies with the local authorities. In recent years, decentralisation has been evident as the responsibilities of local authorities have grown even further while central government has reduced its 'instructions'.

The key incentives to the construction and renovation of social housing are through state loans and rent. Personal housing allowances are also made available to low-income households. Half of all rental stock is state-subsidised social housing, which includes specially designed housing targeted at special needs groups. While the demand for social housing has recently increased, perhaps partly due to the abolition of rent control in unsubsidised housing, cutbacks in capital spending and subsidies have created stagnation in the sector. Moreover, the rate of formation of smaller households has given rise to a demand for small dwellings. Yet in Helsinki in 1996, only 15% of applicants requiring single-room dwellings have been allocated housing. The mismatch between demand and supply has resulted in growing waiting lists and waiting time, especially in larger cities where in-migration has placed further pressures on the housing market. The shortage of affordable rental housing is one of the key reasons for the growth in homelessness especially in light of the free market ideology which has predominated since the 1990s.

Social welfare benefits have been cut considerably which has made it even more difficult for low-income groups to access and maintain decent affordable housing. Reductions in welfare benefits have placed social housing tenants in financial jeopardy by weakening their financial ability to meet rental payments. The result has been a temptation to allocate housing to households with higher income levels who are least likely to fall into rent arrears. Tenants in social housing are at risk of becoming homeless as the threshold for financial acceptability is raised beyond their means.

Sweden

In Sweden (Sahlin, 1998), the 1970s saw a growth in public housing and with it came the closure of men's homes and hostels as people moved into ordinary flats. The reduction in the number of homeless people since the 1970s has further contributed to the decline in traditional hostel, short-term and emergency provision.

However, a significant change in the financing of housing provision occurred in the 1990s which has affected the size of the homeless population. Due to declining finances, local authorities demanded profitability and, as a consequence, public housing agencies have been privatised or simply closed down. Housing subsidies have been severely cut. The ensuing housing shortage has led to an increase in rents, which was compounded by a decrease in the level of benefits paid.

With higher levels of rent and lower levels of benefits, low-income tenants have become increasingly vulnerable to eviction. In fact, eviction rates in Sweden have tripled since the 1980s. This increase in eviction rates has been compounded by the difficulties which poor and previously evicted people experience in accessing housing since public housing agencies have no explicit responsibility to accept tenants perceived as 'risky'. Although the potential for homelessness has increased in recent years, the reality has been, at least partially, alleviated by young people staying in their parents' homes longer and by others doubling up with family and friends.

The housing and social policies of the Nordic states have been broadly characterised by access for all to wide-ranging social security, social welfare and social housing provision. However, budget constraints in recent years have placed greater pressures on the systems and have resulted in severe cutbacks in spending. These cutbacks have affected poor people in two ways: first, the erosion of housing subsidies and the privatisation of existing social rental stock have led to increased demand on diminishing stock. Second, the reduction in benefit levels has meant that fewer people are able to meet the rising cost of housing. Although actual homelessness is not yet a large problem in the Nordic countries, the rise in eviction rates in Sweden, for example, has given cause for concern.

In conclusion then, we can see that the overall European trends outlined above are evident in each of the member states to varying degrees. Demographic changes in the 15 member states have had an impact on the size of the homeless population. These are most notable in the Netherlands, France, Greece, Germany, Belgium, and Spain and, to a lesser extent, Austria. These changes include a growth in the birth rate (the Netherlands and France), immigration and in-migration of foreign workers (Greece, Germany, France, Italy, Spain and Austria), urbanisation (Spain, France), and changes in household size. In the context of these and other processes, variations in housing policy initiatives can be seen to reflect differences between the welfare/housing typologies, between countries within the same social welfare/housing regimes and within some individual states on a regional basis. At the same time, there are some evident similarities between states and between different typologies, the most prominent of which have been driven by the need to limit public expenditure.

Approaches to homelessness

Chapter 1 has discussed the operational definition of homelessness. In this chapter we trace the changing views of homelessness within the member states of the EU. The analysis suggests that there is a shift occurring, within the member states, from a view which posits the nature and causes of homelessness in individual pathological explanations towards socio-structural explanations. Paralleling this shift in attitude is a shift in policy responses from a focus on remedial treatment and control to responses aimed at prevention and reintegration.

This shift in approach can crudely be described, by analogy with the medical and social models of disability, by reference to different models of intervention as outlined in Figure 3.1.

Figure 3.1: Models of intervention for homelessness

Intervention	Police model	Medical model	Social model
Approach	Control	Treatment	Support
Purpose	Curative	Palliative	Preventive

In Italy, the debate on homelessness has focused on the '*senza dimora*' (people of no abode) for whom, it is argued, the absence of housing constitutes one aspect of a wider syndrome of exclusion. The implication for responses to homelessness is that they need to recognise the multi-dimensional nature of the problem and the fact that it is, at least in part, a result of a process of social discrimination. Spain can also be cited, along with Italy, as a country that has made advances, at least in the larger municipalities, in recognising the multi-dimensional nature of homelessness.

In Germany, traditional attitudes to the homeless are still reflected in administrative and legal responsibilities. Thus, although homelessness today is recognised as a structural problem of poverty and lack of housing, the Federal Welfare Act distinguishes between people without a settled way of living, who remain the responsibility of federal welfare institutions, and other homeless people who are the responsibility of the municipalities. Similarly, in Austria homelessness has been recognised as a social problem relatively recently and was, until changes in the legislation in 1974, termed 'non-residency' or vagrancy and treated as a criminal act under police laws.

In Finland, the term homeless people (*koditon*) is seldom used and the Finnish term '*asunnoton*' (literally meaning 'dwellingless' or houseless people) was deliberately introduced in administration and policy in the 1970s. The concept of 'houseless' implies that a person should be helped directly by the provision of housing and other social benefits and thus has a normative policy connotation. The term homeless, on the other hand, reflects the view that the person has no established relationships – 'no one to take care of them'.

In France, Luxembourg and Belgium homelessness has been understood within the dimensions of social exclusion since the 1970s and services have been designed to respond to the global needs of the individual with an emphasis on reintegration or 'reinsertion'.

In Britain, policy responses have, until recently, been structured around the statutory definition of homelessness, while research has consistently emphasised that changes in the supply of and access to housing have been the principal causes of homelessness. Thus, there is an apparent dissonance between the research and policy debates which recognise the structural, intermediate and proximate causes of homelessness and administrative policy responses which have not been focused on a reintegration philosophy.

This changing approach to the conception of homelessness has been underpinned therefore by changes in the perception of the underlying causes of homelessness, which in turn has been reflected in shifts in policy responses in the manner outlined in Figure 2.1 and in service provision (see Chapter 4).

The shift from (larger) institutional forms of provision to smaller and more housing-oriented forms of provision is reported in many countries, although the timing of such changes varies between states. Such trends began in the 1970s in Luxembourg, Germany and the Nordic countries but occurred later in Britain, Austria, Italy and the Netherlands. There is also evidence, in Germany and Finland for example, that with the recent rise in homelessness, there has been a return to more traditional forms of emergency provision though not in the large-scale institutions of the past.

Thus there has been a gradual development towards preventative measures and social reinsertion based on multi-dimensional, integrated approaches. This movement is described typically in Italy where the "first stage of innovation started with criticism of the 'custody' type of traditional intervention based exclusively on remedial approach" (Tosi, 1998, p 11). This process of innovation began in the "second half of the 1970s as a reflection of a more general political and cultural movement which insisted on the de-institutionalisation of social services based on a custody and remedial approach" (Tosi, 1998, p 11). Similar descriptions find echoes in other member states. In Luxembourg it is asserted that "re-integration forms an integral part of the majority of services provided for homeless people" (Pels, 1998, p 45). In Germany in the 1980s a fundamental change of values in the voluntary sector in which integration is taken seriously is reported to have been reflected in legislation (in Article 72 of the Federal Welfare Act).

Approaches to the delivery of services for the homeless also changed as a result of such shifts in thinking. In some countries the trend towards greater coordination and integration of services is enshrined in legislation. Thus in the Netherlands the (44) central municipalities are required, following legislation in 1994, to develop frameworks and policies for integrating services concerning housing, care, employment, poverty and safety. In Finland the Y-Foundation was established in 1985 by the

Association of Finnish Local Authorities, five of the biggest cities, the Finish Red Cross, the Finnish Association for Mental Health, the state alcohol monopoly (ALKO), and the central construction employers and workers union, to provide housing for the 'houseless'. In Austria, on the other hand, the umbrella organisation BAWO is increasingly concerned about the heterogeneous and unregulated nature of service delivery and is actively lobbying for federal legislation for this purpose.

The policy framework: governance and responsibility

Within the context of social welfare reform, deinstitutionalisation and demographic changes, there has been a shift in the nature of responsibility for homelessness within Europe in which it is possible to discern some common trends as well as important differences.

Changes in governance in Europe are well documented elsewhere and have been described to some extent in Chapter 2. In summary, a number of broad trends can be identified which have relevance to this discussion.

Firstly, we can identify a range of legislative changes. These include:

- *Responsibility for homelessness:* Great Britain, uniquely, is the only European state to enshrine statutory responsibility for homelessness [in the 1977 (Housing Homeless Persons) Act] which places specific responsibility on local authorities to rehouse families and other vulnerable people who are 'not intentionally' homeless.
- *Social welfare legislation:* there is a complex and changing pattern of responsibility for homelessness between housing and social work functions within and between member states. This has most commonly involved a shift of responsibility from social work to housing agencies. Examples include the Netherlands where the Welfare Act seeks the integration of housing and welfare policies with other fields of municipal activities; Great Britain where the 1977 Homeless Persons Act shifted responsibility from social work to housing; Luxembourg where three separate ministries are involved; and Ireland where the 1988 and 1992 Housing Acts have enabled voluntary agencies to provide social housing for the homeless.
- *Municipal reform:* there has been an increase in both the powers and responsibilities of local authorities. This includes both giving greater discretionary powers to authorities (for example, in Italy), as well as the creation of new statutory responsibilities (for example, in France and Ireland for assessing need and preparing housing plans).

- *Housing legislation:* additionally, there has been legislative implementation of changes in the role of housing associations and municipal housing companies, which in most cases requires them to operate more as private sector companies rather than as social landlords (for example, in Sweden, Germany, Great Britain and the Netherlands). Among other things, this may mean that allocation is based on criteria other than housing need.

Secondly, we can identify important changes in local governance which include:

- *Decentralisation leading to increasing autonomy for municipalities:* decentralisation of responsibility from central to municipal level of government is a common theme which arises both from a base of municipal reform (for example, the Netherlands, Finland, Sweden and, to some extent, Britain and Ireland) as well as from directives made under statute (Germany, Spain, Austria). It should be clarified that decentralisation of power has not always been accompanied by a commensurate increase in resources to match new responsibilities.
- *Changes in the role of local authorities:* the decentralisation of responsibility to local authorities has often been accompanied by a changing culture of governance. This can be characterised as a shift to the enabling role where the municipality acts as strategic planning and coordinating authority for the local community. This is often accompanied by the adoption of private market mechanisms, which introduce 'quasi-markets' in which the public sector acts as a purchaser of services from the voluntary and private sectors. Such market mechanisms involve processes of competitive bidding as well as the adoption of performance measurement and quality assurance standards. The literature also describes the introduction, in this context, of consumer safeguards, benchmarks or charters. While such trends are not explicitly referred to in the national reports there are examples given of the change in the purchaser–provider split between the public and voluntary sector agencies (in Denmark, the Netherlands, Finland, France, Luxembourg and Ireland, for example).
- *A contractual reliance on non-governmental organisations to provide services:* coupled with these trends to decentralisation and towards an enabling role for local authorities is the increasing role of the voluntary sector as service providers. In all member states voluntary organisations have become the main providers of services for homeless people even where the state also acts as a provider. In some countries this change in role to centre-stage of service provision has occurred

relatively recently, often only since the early 1980s (for example, in Spain, Portugal, Austria, Italy and Ireland).

Diversity in policy and approaches to homelessness

While there are common trends occurring in policy responses to homelessness throughout Europe, there is also diversity reflecting different social, cultural, economic or national circumstances. This diversity occurs both between member states and, importantly, within them. Thus the characteristics which are described above cannot always be assumed to be universally characteristic of the individual countries concerned. Three principal factors can be identified as offering some explanation for this regional disparity.

First, some countries possess distinct legislative structures of government which we may describe as: the federal structure (for example, Austria, Germany, Belgium), regional structure (for example, Spain and, most recently, Britain) and administrative structure (for example, France, Netherlands).

Second, disparity in policy can emerge as a result of the provision by central government of discretionary powers to local authorities. The application of discretionary powers will lead to diversity reflecting different local circumstances as well as different political priorities and administrative capabilities (examples are referred to in Italy, Spain, Portugal and Greece).

Third, regional economic disparities, which are endemic to most member states, result in North–South (Britain, Italy), East–West (Germany), centre–periphery (France) as well as rural–urban (Austria, Finland, Sweden, Ireland, Greece, Spain and Portugal) differences in the application of policies. Indeed, in some countries national legislation is framed specifically to take account of, or to counterbalance, such disparities and inequalities. Equally, some member states adopt regional policies which are framed to take advantage of EU structural fund priorities.

In addition to such factors, it is apparent that some countries demonstrate problems or circumstances which are unique to that country and which are not reflected in transnational trends. Examples of such situations might include countries such as Greece, where the repatriation of citizens from the former Soviet Union (region of Portros) creates a specific problem of homelessness which is exacerbated by the inflow of mainly illegal immigrants, estimated to involve over half a million people. Germany also has experienced the repatriation of citizens from Eastern Europe (the *Ausslieder*) up to the early 1990s and where the inclusion of the former GDR has led to particular problems associated with enlargement and harmonisation.

The significance of these trends in the policy framework and in the changing forms of governance for the provision of services for homeless people, and especially for the innovative capacity of voluntary sector organisations, will become apparent in the following chapters.

FOUR

Innovative services for the homeless

This chapter considers the nature of innovation in services for the homeless as a preliminary to discussion of the developments occurring in the provision of services across Europe. It begins with a consideration of the meaning of innovation with reference to the issues discussed in Chapter 2. An examination of changes in the nature and type of services for homeless people reflects changing policy perceptions of the nature of homelessness itself and this issue is briefly considered. The discussion then moves on to the identification of recent forms of innovation, which may be associated with the emergence of the social model of homelessness, and to an examination of the nature of institutional innovation within the context of the structure–agency model. This analysis is then used to develop a conceptual framework of innovation which is used in Chapters 5, 6 and 7 to examine the nature of innovative services for homelessness in Europe.

The nature of innovation

In Chapter 2 we argued that change and innovation in the delivery of services to the homeless can be classified as 'endogenous' and 'exogenous'; the former reflecting a learning and adaptive process resulting from the 'normal' operation of the systems of service delivery, the latter reflecting more radical changes and innovations resulting from external pressures, in this case fundamental transformations in the social, demographic and economic structures of European society. Innovation, whether endogenous or exogenous, is the product of a 'structuring process' in which proactive agents (including policy makers, social workers and housing managers) working within the context of constraining and permissive structures (traditions, rules and bureaucratic and institutional forms) inherited from the past, make strategic, organisational and operational decisions and choices about the delivery of services. Such choices and decisions can be considered innovative if they can be distinguished from established mainstream forms of assistance; innovation is reflected in imaginative and successful schemes for dealing with the challenge and demands of changed circumstances.

Recent innovations in service delivery to the homeless have been sparked by fundamental social transformations. These changes, encapsulated in the concept of social exclusion, have challenged the capacity and ability of existing welfare and housing regimes to deal with problems of homelessness. Created during periods of low unemployment and traditional family structures, European welfare and housing regimes have found it difficult to respond either to the unprecedented expansion in demand from traditionally targeted groups or to new demands from new groups. Their capacity to respond is frustrated by fiscal restraint on the part of all European states and confounded by recognition that the form and orientation of many of the services presently offered do not adequately tackle the problems of exclusion.

There is now a wide recognition throughout Europe that homelessness, as a component of social exclusion, needs to be seen as more than an absence of shelter. Services to the homeless which contribute to tackling the problem of exclusion are required to be multi-faceted, to be focused on the requirements of individuals and aimed at the prevention of homelessness through permanent (re-)integration. Provision of adequate shelter remains basic, but needs to be tied to a programme of reintegration of homeless individuals or households into mainstream society or a supportive community. Such programmes should break free of uniform institutional provision and be individually tailored to enable the development of social networks through occupational activity and/or community involvement. Reintegration, if it is to be meaningful and permanent, also requires empowerment of homeless people as users of services. User involvement in the design, organisation and running of homeless services becomes a prerequisite for the development of capacities and potential for independent living. This is the reality of the challenge to the development of services for homeless people in *fin de siècle* Europe.

Historical change and innovation in homelessness services

The nature of services for the homeless has been changing over time. Some changes have occurred in response to a change in the perception of homelessness as a socio-structural issue rather than as an issue of personal crisis or individual pathology. Equally, other changes have occurred as a result of the way agents operate in deploying, challenging and potentially transforming resources, rules and ideas as they frame and pursue their own strategies. However we view the underlying causes, the focus of policy has changed over the past four decades: from the 1960s, when the emphasis was on emergency provision in large-scale homeless hostels, through the 1970s and 1980s when the focus shifted to treatment and rehabilitation and, with the development of small-scale supported accommodation in the 1980s, to a growing recognition of the need for long-term and preventative solutions. These changes were a prelude to the emergence in the 1990s of an emphasis on reintegration into permanent housing.

These shifts in approach were described in Chapter 3 by reference to different models of intervention (Figure 3.1). These models of intervention – police, medical and social – have been associated with innovation in the nature and form of services for the homeless during the last 30 years. In reality, however, though the nature of intervention has shifted in the manner suggested, successive policy responses have led to a widening and amalgamation of already existing service forms rather than to their complete replacement by a new generation of service.

From the perspective of a social model (in contrast to that of a police or medical model) the problems of homeless people are seen as multi-dimensional and as requiring services that address a complex of needs. These needs can be broadly defined by reference to a number of policy areas: accommodation, financial support, social or personal support, medical support, employment and training services. The provision of accommodation services may range from the more traditional large-scale emergency hostel forms of accommodation through to family-scale supported accommodation. Financial support services may include provision related to social protection and income support through to direct housing (and related) grants and subsidies. Social support may include the individual support services related to personal needs through to day centres and 'ambulatory' services targeted at groups of people who are homeless or at risk of homelessness. Health services may be associated with the individual's disabilities or dependency on the one hand, and their crisis or short-term needs on the other hand. These services may also be linked to other programmes of reintegration such as training and employment projects. In addition to these services, which are required to meet the prevailing needs of homeless people, it is possible to identify a range of services required to facilitate change in an individual's life situation – these may include advice services, emergency services, assessment and reception services.

The principles which guide service provision today, as enunciated by the social model, may, in more general terms, be described as having the following objectives. First, the provision of emergency treatment and support; second, recognition of the multi-dimensional aspects of the homelessness problem; and third, reintegration. The fulfilment of these objectives is achieved by adopting an approach which facilitates the integration of services (housing, employment, social), individualises casework and permits flexibility of delivery.

Thus we can characterise the range of services for homeless people, evident to different degrees in each EU member state, by means of the four categories in Figure 4.1.

Figure 4.1: Services for the homeless

Approach	Accommodation	Homeless services	Financial services/ support
Emergency/ crisis	Traditional night shelters	Advice/ reception	Income
	Hostels for special groups (ex-offenders, single mothers etc)	Emergency facilities	
		Soup kitchens and clothes stores	
		Medical facilities	
Transitional/ support	Transitional housing		Social support
	Sheltered housing		
	Supported housing		
Permanent/ integration		Work insertion/ training	Employment
	Ordinary housing	Work	Housing

Source: Adapted from Tosi (1998)

Jan Vranken (1997) argues that to combat homelessness, we need a concept in which "general policies, poverty policies and specific homelessness policies are integrated". In this context Vranken defines a number of elements or requirements for homelessness policies which may be summarised as: multi-dimensional, integrated, long-term, preventative, structural and participative.

These elements are used in the following chapters to guide our discussion of innovative services as described in the national case studies (see Appendix).

Innovation: the organisational context

In a recent analysis of the innovative capacity of voluntary organisations, Osborne (1998), building on the work of Abernethy et al (1983), has usefully classified the scope and nature of organisational change in what he refers to as the 'human services'. In this classification, innovative activity is differentiated from developmental activity (Figure 4.2).

Figure 4.2: Organisational change in human services

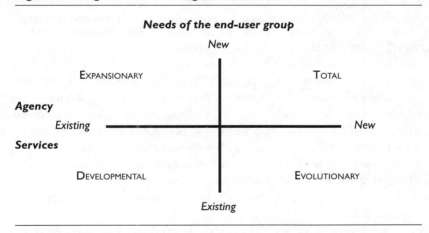

Source: After Osborne (1998)

This approach identifies four different types of change classified in terms of impact on the end-user target group and in terms of the services provided by the organisation:

- *total:* change is both new to the organisation (or may even be the creation of a new organisation) and serves a new target group;
- *expansionary:* change involves offering an existing service of an organisation to a new target group;
- *evolutionary:* change involves providing a new service to the existing target group of an organisation;
- *developmental:* change involves the modification or improvement in the delivery of existing services to an existing target group.

In the context of this study we need to establish those factors that are likely to influence the emergence of innovatory services for the homeless (total change in Osborne's classification) over merely developmental, expansionary or evolutionary change in service provision.

Kleinman (1996), in considering how and why policy development has varied across countries, refers to the concept of 'path dependence' to suggest that countries lock into types of policy regime at a relatively early stage. The reasons for this, he suggests, are likely to be complex – reflecting the balance of class interests and forces, inherited tradition and modes of thought, the influence of particular individuals, politicians, reformers and so forth. The implication is that innovation and adaptation may be prevented or slowed down by established structures, vested interests and habits of working, even in the face of powerful exogenous pressures for change.

In seeking an understanding of the circumstances and conditions which influence the emergence of innovation, the relations between individual agencies and the wider context need to be understood in terms of the interaction between context and process and between structure and agency. In this way we may avoid the simple juxtaposition of descriptive analysis and in so doing highlight the complexities involved in transferring innovatory practices from one policy context to another. This principle has driven our search for a framework (Chapter 2) which is robust enough to describe the nature and causes of innovation within member states and yet provides insights into the wider, transnational, issues which must be understood if innovative practice is to be effectively explained and applied elsewhere.

In addressing this question, of what determines innovatory capacity of individual organisations, Osborne (1998) identifies three clusters of factors – the structural attributes of the service delivery organisations themselves, environmental factors, and the wider institutional context in which individual organisations operate.

In Osborne's research findings, a direct relationship was found between innovative capacity and the external environment of the organisation, whereas the internal structure of the organisation appeared to have little impact on the capacity for innovation. All the non-governmental organisations in Osborne's research sample tended to have low levels of structural complexity and highly informal environments. However, among these, innovative organisations, when compared with more traditional, less innovative organisations, tended to inhabit more complex environments with sophisticated interactive networks of relationships. Additionally, Osborne's research indicates the manner in which conditions at the meta- and macro-level may influence innovation. Our interpretation of his findings would suggest, for example, that legislative changes and emerging (market-led) forms of governance might act to institutionalise innovation as a legitimate activity through the processes of competitive bidding, performance-led funding mechanisms or by initiating demonstration projects specifically to stimulate innovation.

Osborne makes three important points in relation to non-governmental organisation (NGO) innovative capacity: (i) that factors which influence change and innovation do not operate in isolation but rely upon interaction for their import; (ii) that environmental and institutional factors are mediated through a network of external contacts; and (iii) that the innovative activity (or not) of an NGO can influence its future relationships with its institutional and environmental framework. We might also stress the apparent importance of the network of inter-organisational contacts in influencing innovation in service provision. Such networks could, we may assume, be important in several ways: identifying unmet needs, developing new approaches to service delivery, as a route for resource acquisition, or providing a context for implementing new services. In addition, the networks may themselves evolve in response to innovation by, for example, the emergence of primary–secondary relationships where larger (or specialist) organisations provide important services to other organisations in the network.

Many of these issues are apparent in the case studies reported on here and may help to explain the nature (or absence) of innovation. More importantly, they may be suggestive of the circumstances under which innovations may be capable of translation or diffusion to other situations within individual countries or elsewhere in Europe.

Innovative services: an institutional framework of analysis

Given the level of complexity of relations between the different structures, bodies, procedures, and policies involved in the provision of services for the homeless, it is important to be able to make sense of the individual services both in terms of their constituent parts and as part of an interrelated whole.

One way of dealing with this complexity would be to use a framework of analysis which identifies three levels of institutional activity – strategic, organisational and operational – and relate this to the three components of service provision – planning, management and implementation (Figure 4.3).

The strategic level of analysis involves those aspects which affect an organisation's goal and objective setting, strategic planning activities and relationship to its external environment, while the organisational level involves those activities which relate to the management of the resources and activities of an organisation. The operational level of analysis encompasses those activities required to effect changes in the lives of the individuals for whom the services are provided. At each of these levels, activities of planning, management and implementation are involved as outlined in Figure 4.3.

Figure 4.3: An institutional framework of service provision for the homeless

	Planning	**Management**	**Implementation**
Strategic level	• Planning fora • Multi-agency strategies • Research & information • Policy development	• Priorities for investment • Resource management • Government as purchaser of housing services	• Assessing local needs • Evaluating funding applications
Organisational level	• Service planning • Project development • Project design	• Finance • Project management	• Defining needs of user groups • User involvement
Operational level	• Effecting change for individuals • Levels of user satisfaction	• Care planning and management	• Needs assessment

Source: Adapted from Rowley (1995)

In practice, of course, we would not expect the issues to divide so neatly into the boxes of the grid. User involvement and quality assurance, for instance, will cut across all of the boxes. The value of the above schema is as an heuristic device for making sense of the issues, connecting them into a coherent assessable framework within which the nature of innovation may be discussed. Within this framework we recognise that mainstream forms of service or assistance in some countries may be considered innovative in other countries where they have been introduced for the first time. We also recognise that specific efforts to integrate different services for homeless people into mainstream systems of protection may be the most important component of innovation in some countries. We attempt to reflect this in our analysis by including new forms of service provision as innovative in the respective national contexts and thus we relax the paradigm of innovation defined above to take account of divergent social welfare (and housing) regimes.

Using Figure 4.3 as the framework for our analysis of the national case studies, it is possible to identify different forms of innovation in services. First, strategic innovations, which include innovative approaches to coordination between agencies, funding mechanisms, or partnership arrangements. Second, organisational innovations, related to the nature, objectives and purpose of the service which encompass innovations in existing services or the development of new service structures, for example, linking housing and non-housing services as in supported housing projects or in projects linking housing and employment. Third, operational innovations involving new methods of service delivery and implementation, for example, user involvement in service provision and implementation, as well as new forms of living arrangements to meet specific user requirements.

Conclusion

The provision of services for homeless people has been evolving in all European countries in a manner which is typified by a shift from large-scale institutional accommodation and services toward the small-scale and individualised assistance. It has been claimed that this has been associated with a shift in approach from remedial, emergency and treatment-based approaches towards preventative approaches, which in turn has resulted in a move from segmented services to more integrated forms of intervention. Latterly, an increasing emphasis on reintegration programmes has become evident.

These shifts in the form and nature of service provision for the homeless have occurred within the context of changes in social welfare structures which are radically reshaping the external environment in which the organisations providing services for the homeless are operating. It has been argued that changes in the wider environment within which agencies providing services for homeless people operate, point to an important set of factors influencing the innovative capacity (Osborne, 1998) of the public and voluntary organisations involved. These have been described as:

- changes in the role of government and the legislation;
- differentiation of responsibilities, for example, the decentralisation to municipal authorities;
- the development of the purchaser/provider split in the roles of local authorities and voluntary organisations;
- changes in health and social welfare provision leading to deinstitutionalisation;
- diversification of the sociodemographic characteristics of individuals seeking homeless services.

We have also described the changes in attitude and perception of the nature of homelessness, as a social and political problem, which has resulted in recognition of the need to:

- develop a reintegration approach;
- deal with the multi-dimensional facets of homelessness;
- develop an individualised and negotiated approach to service implementation.

The remainder of this report focuses on the detail of the nature of innovation in the provision of services for the homeless. The nature of such innovation – at the strategic level, at the organisational level and at the operational level – needs to be understood, however, in the welfare and housing context in which it occurs. Thus, for example, the introduction of municipal homeless shelters for the first time in Portugal and Greece, represent a degree of innovation in the response of the public sector in those countries even though such services have been developed in other countries for some time.

FIVE

Services for the homeless: strategic innovation

Introduction

We have argued in the previous chapter that the innovative capacity of an organisation is influenced by institutional factors including national legislation and government policy, by external environmental factors, the most important of which involve funding patterns, and by the existence of and the level of development of networks of inter-organisational contacts. Following from this we argue that at the strategic level innovation, when it occurs, is likely to be evident in the three areas of strategic planning, strategic management and in strategic implementation (Figure 5.1).

Figure 5.1: Strategic innovation

	Planning	**Management**	**Implementation**
Strategic level	• Planning fora	• Priorities for investment	• Assessing local needs
	• Multi-agency strategies	• Resource management	• Evaluating funding applications
	• Research and information	• Government as purchaser of housing/ homelessness services	
	• Policy development		

At the strategic planning level, innovation embraces: the development of national or regional research, including pilot projects, to test different policy approaches; the development of partnerships, of networks of agencies or the creation of new agencies designed to assist in the planning and implementation of services.

Innovation at the level of strategic management is manifest in: the introduction of new legislation or guidance; the introduction of (purchaser–provider) funding mechanisms; the shifting of priorities for capital and revenue funding; or the introduction of new mechanisms to improve the efficacy of funding, as well as in the management of funding mechanisms to facilitate or encourage private sector involvement.

Strategic implementation innovation involves the introduction of: new structures of municipal and regional responsibility for homeless services; the allocation of responsibility for the assessment of needs at the regional and local levels; the identification of services required to meet the needs of new target groups; and the implications of reintegration policies for the approach to meeting the needs of existing target groups.

The case studies (see Appendix for details) provide examples of several of these forms of innovation. These include:

At the strategic planning level:
- government funding for innovation in pilot programmes;
- creation of new agencies at national and regional level to plan and coordinate provision;
- the development of coordinating machinery or partnerships to integrate the actions of public and voluntary sector agencies.

At the strategic management level:
- the impact of new legislation leading to innovation in service provision;
- the use of mechanisms designed to increase private sector tenancies for homeless people.

At the strategic implementation level:
- the introduction of responsibility for municipal authorities to provide homeless services;
- the introduction of responsibility for municipal or non-governmental agencies to assess need.

Each of these is considered in turn in the following sections.

Strategic planning

Government funding for innovation in pilot programmes

A number of countries in the EU have invested in pilot programmes with the specific aim of developing innovatory approaches to the problems of homelessness and poor housing. These programmes have been funded variously through social welfare, urban regeneration and housing budgets.

France

In France the Direction Départementale de l'Action Sanitaire et Sociale (DDASS) in La Roche sur Yon has taken the lead in organising and funding a pilot project for a three-year period to network existing services for homeless people (*Case Study 9*, Appendix). As both the funding agency and the leader of the project, the DDASS has shown that effective cooperation between statutory and voluntary sector organisations can empower the voluntary sector by treating them not only as direct service providers but also as equal partners. The mobilisation of political will in the response to issues of homelessness is an important outcome of the project and one which is generally missing from the more common enabler/purchaser role adopted by district authorities. The wide spectrum of agencies involved and the broad rather than specific approach that is being adopted leaves it up to service users to decide on the most appropriate services to meet their needs.

Germany

In Germany the Federal Ministry for Urban Development introduced a major scheme 'Experiments in urban development' (EXWOST) to support the scientific evaluation of seven pilot schemes in seven municipalities throughout Germany. A research project was included within this overall programme to evaluate approaches to the permanent housing provision of homeless people. To be selected for funding the pilot schemes had to demonstrate innovative institutional and financial approaches. The schemes also had to be aimed at the reintegration of homeless people by the provision of normal and affordable housing at normal building standards with regular tenancy agreements and situated in non-stigmatised surroundings. Fifty proposals were considered and seven selected. Between 1994 and 1997 these projects were evaluated in detail at project level and a summary evaluation was also carried out.

Netherlands

In the Netherlands the national government Department of Health, Welfare and Sports has introduced funding for a four-year period for projects aimed at innovative policies in the social and cultural fields in the four main cities (Amsterdam, Rotterdam, The Hague and Utrecht). The project chosen by The Hague focused on people on the margins of social exclusion including drug addicts, ex-offenders, young homeless and ex-psychiatric patients (*Case Study 19*, Appendix). This pilot project was aimed at developing techniques for integrating policies concerning housing, work and welfare. The municipality has established a project office, involving civil servants from each of the different sectors, with responsibility to fund innovative projects by voluntary organisations from a budget of eight million guilders (€3.5 million) and to evaluate the outcomes.

United Kingdom

The Rough Sleepers Initiative (RSI), which began in London in 1990, is funded through the United Kingdom central government Department of the Environment, Transport and the Regions, (formerly the Department of the Environment). Initially for three years, it has subsequently been renewed three times in London and has now been extended to other English towns and to Scottish cities. As the name implies, RSI was established as a response to increasing concerns with the growing number of people sleeping rough on the streets of the capital and other British towns and cities. The initiative offers block grant payments to agencies dealing with the homeless to explicitly target street sleepers, to offer them accommodation in shelters and to work towards their resettlement in temporary or, preferably, permanent housing. Rough sleepers, by definition, are among the most marginalised and vulnerable of the chronically homeless, requiring multiple forms of support as well as shelter. The provision of a block grant funding – a fixed amount of funds which is not dependent on assessment of the individual needs of each resident – permits the development of an holistic, comprehensive approach to resettlement of the chronically homeless, thereby overcoming a major barrier to effective resettlement, namely the difficulty in putting together complex funding packages. Neville House, a winter shelter in London, provides an example of how RSI funding can work in an innovatory and effective manner (*Case Study 25*, Appendix).

A number of shortcomings of the RSI initiative can, however, be identified. First, funding is short term, available in three-year packages and, except in Scotland, covers only revenue and not capital costs. Second, it is clear that the initiative has missed some of the most marginalised and vulnerable, the hard core of the street homeless. This is in part related to the way achievement is assessed. Targets established for each of the funded schemes are all output related. In the Neville House case study, annual targets are set at 8% of residents to be permanently resettled and 36% to be moved to temporary accommodation. In addition, each resettlement worker is required to achieve 35 moves to permanent accommodation each year. With targets so focused on output, the temptation for resettlement workers is to select those who are more likely to contribute to achieving the targets and to ignore the most difficult cases. It is questionable as to whether targets of this type should be applied to chronically homeless people with complex and multiple needs. More appropriate targets need to be devised, using more meaningful criteria based, for example, on staged progress towards resettlement.

While pilot projects, such as those cited above, can be important stimulants for innovative activity in, for example, the development of policies and appropriate funding mechanisms as well as in evaluating funding applications from the voluntary sector, there are important questions in relation to their use. The above examples are illustrative of pilot initiatives that have emanated from different sectors of government and have been associated, variously and separately, with urban regeneration programmes, with social welfare policies and with housing policies. They sometimes lack overall coherence and their wider and longer-term applicability to the development of sustainable reintegration policies and services for homeless people is possibly questionable. While such pilot projects may be successful over a defined period by virtue of their ability to concentrate skills, effort and resources to a specific area or problem, by redirecting effort and resources, they can have the effect of distorting the development of existing initiatives. Unless there is explicit and determined effort to evaluate such schemes from their inception, using both qualitative and quantitative indicators, then the potential for the diffusion of such innovation will remain uncertain. Yet pilot projects may have an important role in helping to build organisational contacts and partnerships which, as our analytical framework suggests, are vital to the development of innovative activity.

Creation of new agencies

A legitimate response by organisations to changes in the external environment is the creation of new structures or agencies. Such responses have been evident in a number of member countries since the early 1980s. There are examples of new agencies coming into existence at national, regional and local levels in response to changes in government policies, increasing levels of homelessness and the recognition of a more diverse range of needs. Such new agencies may be developed in response to government initiative (as, for example, in the Netherlands), in reaction to government legislation (Austria and Denmark), in response to the initiative of a key agency (Finland), in response to a crisis or scandal (Britain), or by the combined actions of public and/or voluntary agencies (for example, in Italy and Greece).

The functions of the newly created agencies differ depending on a number of factors, including the reason for their creation, the state of development of other agencies and the nature of the problem they aim to address.

Belgium

In Belgium activities by welfare and tenant organisations in Flanders have led to the creation of a new umbrella organisation, Vlaams Overleg Bewonersbelangen (VOB) (Flemish Forum for Residents' Interests), to coordinate the work of a wide range of housing initiatives (*Case Study 5*, Appendix). The umbrella organisation was established in the light of research that highlighted the lack of coordination and the ineffective use of multi-disciplinary approaches in addressing the needs of homeless people. It showed that such services were fragmented, inefficient, unprofessional and plagued by management problems such as high staff turnover. In response, VOB offers to its members training, management support, and monitoring, logistic support for campaigning, lobbying and the stimulation of new network creation. The importance of its work with Social Rental Agencies (SVKs) has spurred the Flemish regional government to sign a convention with the umbrella group and to recognise and subsidise the work of the SVKs themselves through legislation. Apart from the SVKs, the VOB also covers the work of tenant organisations, organisations for community work and organisations working with special target groups. A donation from Caritas of 500,000 BEF (€12, 500) helped to secure VOB's initial activities.

Finland

A nationwide organisation, the Y-Foundation, was established in Finland in 1985 to provide housing for the homeless and for refugees (*Case Study 8*, Appendix). The agency was founded by the Association of Finnish Local Authorities, five of the biggest Finnish cities, the Finnish Red Cross, the Finnish Association for Mental Health, the state alcohol monopoly (ALKO), and the central construction employers and workers unions. The Foundation operates in close partnership with the public sector and other NGOs. Financial assistance is provided for the purchase of housing by the state, the Slot Machine Association, and local authorities with which the Foundation has links, as well as by low-interest state loans and bank loans. The role of the Foundation is to act as a real estate and property management agency working on the principle of purchasing small apartments of a good standard from the existing housing stock. The dwellings (4,600 purchased to date in 46 municipalities) are placed at the disposal of the local authorities and church congregations, which select the occupants and provide support services as required.

Germany

In 1989 the first plans were made to open a central housing agency within the voluntary sector in Hanover, Germany, in response to the trends in the increase in homelessness and to the difficulties of rehousing single homeless people in normal, permanent housing. For administrative and management purposes a new special department of the Central Advice Office of the Diakonisches Werk (a Protestant welfare association acting on a municipal and national level) was set up. This new department called, the Soziale Wohnraumhilfe (SWH), was intended initially to be a pilot scheme, operating for five years (*Case Study 12*, Appendix). A specific function of SWH was to demonstrate the feasibility of integrating the single homeless into normal, permanent housing. In order to achieve this aim, SWH took on the risks of administration and management by renting the dwellings and sub-letting them to single homeless people. SWH cooperates with different services and institutions to provide care and support to the tenants; the landlord role of SWH is thereby kept separate from the provision of support to individual tenants. Thus SWH functions as a classic mediator, facilitating communication and cooperation between different agents to achieve a desired result – the integration of homeless people into permanent housing.

The above examples illustrate the importance of new agencies in initiating innovative developments in service provision through the introduction of new ideas, new mechanisms for coordination of resources and new structures for service delivery. While governments can stimulate the creation of new agencies, their evolution and successful development often depends on a positive reaction from the voluntary sector to government policy and on the development of inter-organisational contacts. The following examples demonstrate the significance of having national or regional umbrella organisations which can both engage with government at the strategic planning level on behalf of service providers

and achieve the economies of scale and expertise necessary to utilise private sector financial sources.

The development of coordinating structures, networks or partnerships

A key principle of the approach to service provision for homelessness, which has emerged during the last 20 years, is the recognition of the multi-dimensional nature of the problems which homeless people present. If effective reintegration policies are to be developed, then it is necessary that issues of support, income and employment, as well as accommodation, are simultaneously addressed. This presumes the need, therefore, to integrate the activities of relevant agencies in each of these fields. The nature of this integration can vary from relatively low level cooperation through to the more detailed coordination of policies and procedures, to the actual establishment of network or partnership arrangements dealing with specific problems or a specific geographical area. Eventually, such cooperation could lead to the creation of totally new agencies or to the merger of existing agencies. There are examples across Europe of interagency cooperation and coordination aimed at integrating policy responses to homelessness and there are also examples of emerging partnerships focused on the management of specific initiatives or projects.

Austria

In Austria, the Wohnplattform Linz project (*Case Study 1*, Appendix) originated from an informal working group of social workers employed by a variety of regional institutions. These individuals were drawn together by a common interest in resolving the difficulties of identifying and maintaining housing for their clients. Aware that interagency competitiveness and scant resources create tensions in accessing housing, the group decided to form a collaborative and cooperative network to pool resources and reduce competition. The project, established in 1984, is founded on the Upper Austrian Law relating to housing, which provides a legal basis for interagency cooperation and allows for preferential treatment of social services providers in obtaining leases for rental properties.

France

The project at La Roche sur Yon (Vendée) began in France in 1995 with, as a key objective, the organisation and networking of existing services in the area to provide service users with a diverse yet integrated series of options to meet their various and complex needs (*Case Study 9*, Appendix). Focusing on the empowerment of the service users, the project not only explicitly involves users in decision making with regard to the choice of services appropriate to their needs, but also involves them as active partners in specific elements of the work. A wide range of agencies, both statutory and voluntary, are involved in the project. It operates as a loosely constructed partnership with the DDASS (Direction Départementale de l'Action Sanitaire et Sociale), taking the lead in the creation of the project and the coordination of the day reception centre. The mobilisation of statutory agencies such as the DDASS, the Caisse d'Allocations Familiales (CAF) and the Centre Communal d'Action Sociale, (CCAS), is of particular interest since it signals a departure from the norm in France where statutory agencies are seldom inclined to work in true partnership with voluntary sector agencies or with housing associations. In this instance, a broader interpretation of legislative frameworks for the delivery of services has enabled statutory agencies to become real partners.

Ireland

In Ireland no central government department has direct responsibility for the homeless. Under the terms of the 1988 Housing Act and the 1991 Child Care Act some responsibility was attributed respectively to local authorities and to regional health boards. A range of voluntary agencies – church-based and private – provide the bulk of homeless services in the form of large, recently renovated institutional hostels in which self-contained accommodation is increasingly available and in the form of purpose-built shelters. There has been a belated recognition of the inadequacy of funding and regulation on the part of central government as a consequence of increasing evidence of homelessness, especially in Dublin and other cities, and vociferous campaigning on the part of voluntary organisations. In response to the issue of increasing homelessness in Dublin, the Minister of State at the Department of the Environment in October 1996 established a unique initiative to coordinate the work of statutory agencies and voluntary providers of services to the homeless. Under the terms of the initiative, new arrangements are being put into place to provide a framework for a more cooperative and unified approach by statutory authorities, working with the voluntary sector, to plan and coordinate the development and delivery of services to the homeless. The lack of effective coordination between the Eastern Health Board and the local authorities in the Dublin region had long been identified as a major impediment to the provision of an adequate and comprehensive range of services. Emphasis, under this initiative, is placed on the planned development and delivery of services that embrace flexibility amid consultation and coordination. Specifically the initiative aims to improve knowledge of services, of gaps in services and in delivery structures and organisation and to improve contact and trust between all agencies working with the homeless in order to develop a better understanding of the benefits of partnership. In addition, the initiative has commissioned research on the potential for information technology in service provision and coordination, the impact of asylum seekers on housing services of the future and on the development of indicators with the aim of developing standards of performance for each agency and to enable effective monitoring. The main priority of the initiative is, however, to develop a viable settlement strategy which will facilitate movement of homeless people from emergency, temporary accommodation to permanent stable and secure accommodation of appropriate standard and to establish a transparent funding regime especially with regard to securing support services (*Case Study 16*, Appendix).

Italy

The present San Marcellino project in Italy (*Case Study 17*, Appendix) began in 1986 with the aim of providing diversified services for seriously marginalised homeless people (of no abode – *senza dimora*) based on individual case plans. To achieve this aim, the project involves coordination with public and voluntary sector agencies and the development of flexible and long-term solutions based on individual care plans. San Marcellino cooperates with a range of agencies – including Caritas (Centro Monastero), which operates a similar service; the local authority (night) shelter (referrals); CAD (public sector social services for elderly people/rent subsidy); mental health services (joint casework plans); the local authority Solidarity Office (finance) – in an attempt to provide an integrated service. A Technical Operational Group, consisting of representatives from the district social services offices, the municipal shelter, San Marcellino and Caritas, has been established with the aim of defining responsibilities and finding common methods of working. Thus the innovation may best be described as adopting a network approach rather than a partnership approach.

Luxembourg

In Luxembourg, Wunnengshellef (*Case Study 18*, Appendix) was commissioned by the Ministry of the Family in order to act as a central housing negotiation service enabling member associations, who provide short-term accommodation and/or support services, to move clients on to more long-term accommodation with continuing support. Because Wunnengshellef is responsible for identifying, preparing and managing housing while the member agencies are responsible for support services and referrals, a wider range of client groups with diverse needs can have access to housing in a more cost-effective way. By working cooperatively, each member agency can both contribute its expertise and share a common understanding of the multi-dimensional characteristics of homelessness. The involvement of private and public sector landlords in the project also helps to raise their awareness of issues of homelessness while maximising the use of existing resources.

These examples of innovation in strategic planning through the creation of new agencies illustrate issues relating to the mechanisms which, on the one hand, facilitate the development of coordination and, on the other hand, are necessary to allow its effective operation. It is clear that innovation in coordination can occur as a reaction to a problem, in response to government intervention, or result from the initiative of voluntary organisations. However, there are an important and, we suspect, increasing number of government-driven initiatives whereby voluntary organisation coordination and networks emerge in response to funding practices based on competitive bidding and provider–purchaser mechanisms of control.

Strategic management

The impact of new legislation

There are several examples of changes in legislation leading to innovation in service provision, either as the result of organisations having to adapt to new regulations requiring the execution of new statutory duties, or as a result of the creation of new sources of funding.

Belgium

In 1993, legislation was introduced in Belgium (Wallonia) aimed at recognising and financing the work of the Social Rental Agencies (SRAs). This legislation was driven by the recognition of both the shortage and poor condition of affordable housing and the inability of the existing social housing sector to meet a growing demand for such housing (*Case Study 3*, Appendix). The legislation, which was amended in 1996, mandated the SRAs to act as mediators between private and public sector landlords and people in need of housing. It also mandated the SRAs to organise social support services in line with individual needs. The aim of the legislation is to maximise the use of existing housing stock and to encourage otherwise reluctant landlords to participate in this critical area of housing provision. The amendments of 1996, which extended the SRAs throughout Wallonia, established the mechanisms by which SRAs can negotiate and formalise contracts and the terms of tenancies. Although SRAs existed prior to 1993, the new legislation has increased the number of SRAs operating in Wallonia and has extended their geographical coverage.

Denmark

Paragraph 105 of Denmark's 1976 Social Assistance Act identifies the responsibilities of the counties and the two municipalities of Copenhagen and Roskilde for the homeless. Initially these responsibilities merely required the provision of temporary shelter. Recent legislative changes (L-8) passed in January 1995 have, however, extended this remit. First, the responsibilities of the counties and the municipalities were extended to cover not only homeless families (that is, households with more than one person) but also single persons. In addition, these responsibilities have been extended to include not only those who are without shelter, but also those who might be in need of shelter as the result of drug abuse or mental illness. This is in line with the adoption in Denmark of a changing definition of homelessness as a facet of social exclusion. Second, the ability of the municipalities to establish shared dwellings as a stage in a process of reintegration was widened from a narrow focus on mentally ill and physically disabled people, to embrace all residents of Paragraph 105 institutions. The legislation also permits the municipalities to provide support and assistance to the occupants of shared dwellings. Third, the responsibilities of the municipalities have been extended to include assessment of the need for and, as appropriate, the development of reintegration programmes after three months' residence in Paragraph 105 institutions. The reintegration programmes have several dimensions: the provision of a contact/support worker for homeless individuals from outside the Paragraph 105 institutions and the establishment of shared dwellings as an alternative to those institutions for both permanent residence and as a transitional form of residence prior to full integration. In addition, direct movement to individually tenanted flats is favoured for 'suitable' individuals. In securing alternative accommodation, the municipalities have nomination rights with non-profit housing organisations as well as, on a more limited basis, with the private sector.

Netherlands

The Netherland's Social Welfare Act of 1994 led to the stimulation of innovation in funding structures. Since 1994, specific financial means were given to 44 city centre authorities making them responsible for developing frameworks and policies for the integration of services concerning housing, care, employment, poverty and safety. In addition, the TWSSV (temporary law on stimulating social innovation), which came into force in January 1994, decentralised responsibility for shelter and care from national to 48 central local authorities. Since that date, these local authorities have been responsible for developing and implementing social policies and its funding, including innovation and prevention and quality assurance.

In these examples, legislative and funding responsibilities are created through social welfare legislation rather than through housing or specifically homelessness legislation. Britain, alone of the European member states, possesses national legislation on homelessness. The implications of this social services focus to legislative innovation for the development of a coherent (and non-departmental) strategy on homelessness are worthy of further examination.

Mechanisms to increase private sector tenancies for homeless people

An important innovation in service provision, in the context of objectives of reintegration, is the attempt to increase the involvement of the private sector in service provision. This may include attempts to introduce private sector finance (which is discussed elsewhere – see Chapter 6) or to encourage or facilitate private landlords to make housing available for homeless people on the basis of normal secure tenancies. In the light of the changes occurring in the reduction of social housing and in the tenure structure of most European states, the successful reintegration of homeless people into the housing market is likely to rely in the future more heavily on maximising the use of private sector housing.

Examples of situations where municipal and voluntary organisations take over the liability for tenancies in order to provide security to private or voluntary landlords, in respect of anti-social behaviour or financial losses arising from rent arrears or necessary repairs, are described in the following case studies.

Belgium

In Belgium, two different Social Rental Agencies (Gestion-Logement-Namur and Charleroi-Logement) work with private landlords to provide housing for families in need of affordable housing and who may have other special needs. Working within the context of the Walloon legislation governing SRAs, these two organisations negotiate short-term renewable tenancies with private sector landlords and then sub-let them to families. Two types of landlords have been involved in the projects: those with a large stock which is difficult to manage and those who have previously had bad experiences with certain types of tenants. The services of the SRAs are offered to the landlords on the basis of a contract, whereby the mediating agencies take 15% of the rent in return for guaranteeing rental income even during void periods and taking on all the risks associated with housing management. Individualised support plans are organised on a needs-led basis and delivered by other specialist service providers with whom the SRAs cooperate. In some cases, where the state of the proposed accommodation is below the acceptable standard, prospective tenants are coopted to undertake renovation work; such work is seen as training, especially for young people (*Case Study 3*, Appendix).

Luxembourg

Wunnengshellef in Luxembourg (*Case Study 18*, Appendix) is an '*association of associations*' and, as such, aims to work with a wide range of agencies to facilitate access to long-term, though not permanent, housing. In the Luxembourg context, this aim is unique since all other providers offer short-term or emergency provision. The cooperative approach adopted means that the member associations can make referrals to Wunnengshellef and, once the referred person is accommodated, the referring agencies undertake to provide an individualised support package. For its part, Wunnengshellef acts as an intermediary, negotiating tenancies with landlords in the public and private sectors which it then sub-lets to clients. As the principal tenant, Wunnengshellef takes on all housing management responsibilities. The involvement of private sector landlords in social housing provision is not unusual within the Luxembourg context, but partnership with private sector landlords in order to provide long-term housing solutions for homeless people is innovative. It is the effective and established cooperative network on which Wunnengshellef is founded which gives landlords the confidence to participate in this type of provision, knowing that the client's special needs will be supported and that the housing management is well in hand.

France

In the Relais Soleil Tourquenois project in Lille in northern France, accommodation is rented by the association either from Habitations à Loyer Modérées (HLMs) or from a private landlord. Rent is paid through various benefit mechanisms and residents become sub-tenants. Eventually, a tenancy can be transferred directly to the tenant in their own right and the association asks the HLM or private landlord for a replacement property. This model allows for a more effective packaging of integration initiatives and shortens the time required to accede to permanent housing. It suppresses the successive ruptures in provision, which are evident in the more classic model where residents have to make several moves before finally settling into permanent accommodation (*Case Study 11*, Appendix).

These examples of innovations designed to increase private sector involvement demonstrate that the provision of guaranteed rentals or the absorption of the risks of housing management may be an effective means of ensuring the provision of accommodation for homeless people – especially those who require support to sustain a tenancy. This approach may, intuitively, be more cost-effective than direct housing provision and may, indeed, be the only option in situations where public sector capital finance or housing stock is restricted. In addition to these examples of increased private sector involvement, there is evidence from Germany that in the social housing sector, too, landlords are by no means automatically willing to take homeless people as tenants and similar 'protected market segment' and 'guaranteed dwellings' schemes are used for the same purpose in conjunction with social housing agencies.

Strategic implementation

The introduction of responsibility for municipal authorities to provide homeless services

Elsewhere in this report we have described the development of service provision as a shift from emergency provision to the provision of services aimed at treatment (of the factors thought to cause homelessness), to solutions based on concepts of social support and individual empowerment. However, it is clear that such a description of development is more familiar to some social welfare regimes than it is to others. In some countries the introduction of services for homeless people for the first time, provided by public agencies, is itself innovative and can lead in turn to changes in the role and function of voluntary and church-based organisations.

There are examples quoted in the case studies of situations where municipal authorities provide shelters for homeless people for the first time (for example, Athens), where municipal authorities create departments with responsibility for the coordination of homeless services (for example, in Vienna) and there are examples of municipal authorities cooperating for the first time with voluntary organisations to effect particular forms of service provision (for example, Lisbon).

Greece

Within the Greek context, local authority involvement in service provision for homeless people, whether directly or indirectly, is innovative (*Case Study 15*, Appendix). The recognition by the Athens City Council of the growing problem of homelessness in the city has led to the creation of a three-phase programme to meet the expressed needs. The first two phases of the project, which started in 1996, involve the provision of, first, a day centre and, second, a transitional accommodation unit. The third phase, due to have started in 1998, aims to include a reintegration programme focused on labour market reinsertion. Although the services are offered on a temporary basis with specific criteria for admission, the fact that such a service has been envisaged, planned and funded (with the exception of phase three) by the City Council demonstrates a growing recognition of the importance of the issue of homelessness and, very importantly, the commitment of local authorities in meeting the needs, however temporarily.

Portugal

The influence of European funding initiatives is highlighted in the Portuguese experience. Action undertaken by the public sector has traditionally focused on the alleviation of the symptoms of deprivation, and less on the root causes of poverty (lack of resources) and exclusion (social links). However, in the early 1990s, largely under the influence of the third European programme to combat poverty, there emerged a recognition of the need to develop a multi-dimensional approach to poverty and homelessness. A project (*Case Study 21*, Appendix) attempting to meet these objectives has been established in the city of Lisbon. Led by the municipality, it involves two non-profit organisations: Foundation for International Medical Assistance (AMI) and the Association of Christian Fraternity (O Campanheiro). The municipality provides the shelter, some technical assistance and funding, AMI manages the shelter and assists with reintegration through counselling, while O Campanheiro assesses clients for job training.

There is now evidence of state involvement in the provision of services for homeless people in all the member states. The examples above illustrate both an acceptance by the state of responsibility for homeless problems and suggest that, at municipal level at least, the state is taking responsibility for coordinating services for homeless people. Implicit in this analysis is the changing conception of the causes of homelessness as described in Chapters 2 and 3.

The introduction of responsibility for municipal or non-governmental agencies to assess need

One of the most underdeveloped areas of policy and service provision is in the area of the assessment of needs. In part this revolves around the lack of available and consistent data on homelessness in most member states and, in part, it reflects on the lack of statutory responsibility for assessing need. There are, however, some examples where national or municipal government has introduced such responsibility in recent years.

Finland

In Finland, the importance of adequate knowledge began to be emphasised in the late 1970s. Housing, welfare and health authorities were urged at that time to collaborate in collecting statistics by, for example, keeping confidential registers. The aim was to make the problem visible for policy makers at both local and central government level. The National Housing Board issues instruction on the collection of information. In 1986 questions about the extent of homelessness were added to the annual housing market surveys undertaken by the municipalities. These surveys form the basis for allocating resources including state loans and allowances for social housing to the municipalities. *Case Study 8* (see Appendix) demonstrates the role of the Y-Foundation, in cooperation with social welfare and healthcare authorities, in assessing the need for supported housing in each municipality.

Ireland

In Ireland, while there is still no central government department with overall responsibility for homelessness, the 1988 Housing Act attributed to local authorities for the first time responsibility for homeless people. In addition, the 1991 Child Care Act assigned primary responsibility for the provision of accommodation for homeless children (up to 18 years) to regional health boards. The responsibilities of the local authorities include the compilation of statistical assessments of the numbers of homeless people in their administrative regions and the provision of accommodation through rehousing in council stock or in conjunction with approved voluntary authorities.

These examples illustrate several important aspects of the difficulty of assessing need. Firstly, clear responsibility and coordination is required to ensure the collection of consistent and accurate information. Secondly, such activity must be continuous by providing frequent survey data that can be relied upon for resource allocation. Thirdly, the nature and form of the information which is collected must be tailored to the manner in which such information will be used; for example, ensuring that housing information is compatible with and can be linked with social care and health information at appropriate levels of aggregation.

Conclusion

Strategic level innovation has been a significant feature of the introduction of new mechanisms of service provision for the homeless. Change has occurred, as the evidence here suggests, following change in the conception of the causes and nature of homelessness and has, in part, been dependent on changes in governance including legislative change and the emerging enabling role of local authorities in the 1980s. Central governments have played a role especially in funding pilot projects aimed at stimulating innovation and reintegration. However, without adequate resources, particularly of revenue funding, it is difficult to see how the diffusion of such innovatory practice will occur. As the literature suggests, innovation requires strong networks of inter-organisational contacts to be effective (see Chapter 4). It is therefore not surprising that there is evidence of partnerships and networks emerging or developing in many member states. The creation of new agencies and of agencies with an umbrella function is a logical development of coordination but is not, on the evidence here, a replacement for effective inter-organisational networks. A reaction of the private market, to competition and the drive for efficiency, has been to develop larger organisations with more diverse functions operating in an oligopoly situation. There is as yet little evidence of mergers occurring from partnership structures and only limited evidence of the development of primary–secondary relationships where larger organisations provide services to smaller agencies. Some forms of innovation are more characteristic of some welfare regimes. For example, the emergence of a role for the public sector in providing services and in coordinating activity with non-profit organisations is a feature of the Mediterranean welfare regimes, while the use of mechanisms to increase the role of private sector housing for reintegration of homeless people is, as we might expect, more common in those countries with a restricted social housing sector.

SIX

Services for the homeless: organisational innovation

Introduction

The institutional framework (Figure 4.3), adopted for the purpose of this report, suggests that innovation may occur in relation to any of the three dimensions of planning, management or implementation. Thus, at the organisational level of analysis, innovation may occur in the design or development of new services or new methods of delivering or combining existing services. Equally, it may occur in relation to the management or financing of services. Or it may involve the extension of services to new client groups, the development or adaptation of services to meet the changing needs of existing users or the involvement of users in the design and implementation of services (Figure 6.1).

Figure 6.1: Organisational innovation

	Planning	Management	Implementation
Organisational level	• Service planning • Project development • Project design	• Finance • Project management	• Defining needs of user groups • User involvement

At the organisational planning level, for most member states, innovation is likely to involve the inclusion of reintegration objectives in the planning of services. Innovation may occur through the targeting of services designed to meet the specific and changing needs of individual client groups, or the development of services to meet the needs of client groups with particularly challenging behaviour, or groups at risk of marginalisation that have not formerly been recipients of services.

Innovations in organisational management include changes in the structures, procedures and organisation of services, or their financing, in order to meet the needs of existing client groups or to include new client groups, in relation to objectives of social integration. The nature of innovation at this level can most readily be observed in the integration of services – housing, welfare, employment and health – which reflect the multi-dimensional nature of homeless problems. Efficient project management in this context will frequently involve innovative efforts to develop services, which maximise the use of financial regulations, involving the utilisation of public and private sector finance in an efficient and cost-effective manner.

Innovation at the level of organisational implementation reflects the need for organisations to develop structures and procedures which allow them to be responsive to changing user needs and to be able to review their services to be responsive to user satisfaction. Such innovations are manifest in the development of services that are flexible and respond to changing user requirements, in the development of services that reflect user needs, and in the development of services that are effective and cost-efficient.

The national case studies provide examples, in almost all countries, of innovations at the organisational planning level. These include projects, developed mainly during the 1990s, which have the specific aim of:

- the reintegration of homeless and long-term homeless people into permanent affordable housing with normal tenancy rights;
- providing for the needs of specific target groups including groups for whom services had not previously been available in their country.

The need for service provision to respond to the multi-dimensional facets of the problems of homeless people is most clearly to be seen in developments at the level of organisational management; examples from the case studies include innovative projects designed to:

- introduce or improve the integration of services including housing, welfare and work;
- use funding mechanisms through the development of a 'service agency' model of operation.

The national case studies provide evidence that, whether in response to changing professional beliefs and organisational values or to the expectations and restrictions of funding providers, organisations are developing at the level of organisational implementation, innovative approaches to service provision which:

- aim to provide flexibility through offering a range of options to meet different and often complex needs;
- develop mechanisms of review and evaluation which will allow the agency to learn and adapt and be responsive to changing user requirements or to new and emerging needs.

In the remainder of this chapter we draw on the national case studies to reveal the nature of innovation in relation to each of the dimensions of organisational planning, organisational management and organisational implementation.

Organisational planning

Reintegration objectives

The evidence from the case studies illustrates the fact that organisations have responded to the desire to reintegrate people into normal and non-stigmatised permanent housing in two distinctive ways. They have responded to the factors which have in part excluded people from the housing market by absorbing and thus minimising the risks to private and social landlords. This has been described above (Chapter 5) in relation to the strategic planning of services. Additionally, they have recognised that people who have led chaotic life-styles or have had long experience of institutional living, will require the provision of individual care and support to enable them to sustain a tenancy and to live independently in the community.

The main form of innovative activity cited by the case studies in relation to the aim of reintegrating homeless people into permanent housing with normal tenancies is best described as 'supported housing'. This form of innovation has occurred both as the result of a single agency providing the housing and support de novo and of housing and support agencies cooperating to enable people to live independently by providing the necessary support to enable them to sustain their tenancies. Examples of such innovation from Denmark, Finland, Germany and Spain are outlined below.

Denmark

The Gå Ud Projekt in Copenhagen, Denmark (*Case Study 6*, Appendix) is slightly different from other supported housing projects described in the case studies in the sense that it is an outreach project associated with a men's shelter. The innovation involved in this case is a resettlement programme associated with the *Mændenes Hjem* emergency shelter financed by a pool scheme under the Ministry of Social Affairs. The project involves the establishment of a full-time support worker attached to the shelter with the specific responsibility of encouraging and assisting the resettlement of residents into a home of their own. This includes assistance in finding suitable accommodation, furnishing it, and obtaining the finance to pay for it and in the provision of necessary aftercare support.

Finland

The Y-Foundation in Finland (*Case Study 8*, Appendix), which has been operating since 1985, has provided over 4,600 apartments in 46 municipalities. Yet it is only since 1994 that it has begun to provide housing support services in cooperation with the Finnish Association of Mental Health, the Association for Relatives and Friends of Mental Health Rehabilitees and the Helmi Mental Health Association. This supported housing is aimed at mental health rehabilitees and persons in danger of marginalisation who cannot cope alone in the community. One particular target group, apart from those with mental illness, is young people with a background of institutional care.

Germany

The Wohnung statt Heimplatz project in Bielefeld, Germany (*Case Study 13*, Appendix) was developed following the decision to reduce the size of a traditional (95-place) homeless institution (to 69 places). To compensate for this loss of accommodation, 24 flats were constructed in three development projects. One of the objectives quoted for the project was to show that extensive social integration is possible even after many years of homelessness and despite a low capacity for self-help. The decision was made at the outset of the project by the agency responsible to separate responsibility for the landlord role and the support services.

Spain

In Spain the Zaragoza Centre for Integration (*Case Study 23*, Appendix), 'Torre Virreina', managed by Caritas, is a small-scale project designed to provide intensive individual support to promote independent living through a carefully devised step-by-step programme of preparation. *Step One*, lasting for three to four months, involves the acquisition of basic social and hygiene skills as part of the process whereby the residents learn to take care of themselves and how to live alongside others. There is a focus on the promotion of self-esteem and self-motivation. A daily allowance is paid and all residents engage in daily cleaning activities as well as individual pursuits; they also participate in self-help group sessions, a social skills workshop and occupational activities for the acquisition of minimum work habits. Cultural activities and general learning are promoted. Work is begun on the preparation of a personal plan for achieving integration. *Step Two*, the take-off phase lasting between six and eight months, is the central plank of the integration process. The focus is on development and completion of the personal reintegration plan and on introducing external activities such as training with the aid of professional institutes, on occupational activities and activities involving relationships with other people inside and outside the Centre. Problem solving and therapy sessions are also introduced. *Step Three*, the exit phase, has a maximum duration of three months; a time limit designed to avoid dependency. As a preparation for leaving the Centre and entering the outside world a subsidised shared flat, attached to the Centre, is provided. Here residents are encouraged and aided in the development of the skills of self-management of personal activities and job seeking. Many of the activities of Step Two, such as group sessions, are continued. With the help of the Parish, an independent flat is eventually found and the resident of the Centre is relocated.

These examples illustrate that various types of support are required for different client groups and for different reasons. The example of outreach support provision (*Gå Ud*, Denmark) is a reminder that some people who have not been used to independent living will require support simply to enable them to sustain a tenancy. Indeed, as we have seen, this may be a necessary corollary to increasing the amount of private sector accommodation for such groups in society. Support is also necessary for young people who have been in care during their childhood or who may have left home under duress, as the Finnish case study illustrates. In addition, supported housing is being developed and introduced to replace institutional forms of living for people who, in the examples shown here, may have a learning disability or mental illness.

Target groups

The institutional framework adopted in this work to facilitate the analysis and description of innovative activity by providers of services for homeless people, suggests that one form of innovation could include the extension of services to new markets or target groups or the development of services to focus on the needs of a specific target group. Indeed, there is evidence in the case studies both of the provision of services specialising in the needs of specific target groups as well as of projects aimed at groups for whom services had not previously been available in their country.

Finland

In Finland, for example, the Jyvaskyla Street Mission (*Case Study 7*, Appendix) is a member of the Finnish Blue Band, which has 66 member associations throughout the country specialising in working with people with substance abuse problems. While much of the activity of the Mission in providing accommodation for substance abusers cannot fairly be called innovative in itself (indeed the Mission has been operating since the 1950s), specialisation in service provision for problems such as substance abuse, can allow agencies to respond to changing needs. For example, as alcohol addiction is replaced by drug addiction as the major substance abuse problem specialist skills can be employed to provide new methods of service delivery. This is especially important where drug addiction remains a criminal activity. Equally, the ability to support people while recognising the impossibility of rehabilitation (for some) requires particular approaches and organisational goals.

France

In France the Association Nivernaise d'Acceuil et de Reinsertion (ANAR, *Case Study 10*, Appendix) targets people who have been in trouble with the law and those who have been excluded from the labour market. The project aims to prevent patterns of re-offending through a balanced and locally sensitive programme of vocational training. The emphasis of the project is on employment, although facilitating access to housing is part of the service. Both men and women participate in the project but the work initiatives are segregated on gender lines with men involved in forestry work and women working in a sewing workshop.

Greece

In Greece, Arsis (*Case Study 14*, Appendix) targets its services exclusively at young people under the age of 21 and, within this group, the focus is on juvenile offenders and those with social dysfunction problems. The services provided include limited accommodation, vocational training and a range of social support services. Arsis' work with this target group is unique in the Greek context since no other providers, either statutory or voluntary, deal with this client group. In fact, the ethos and philosophy of choice and empowerment is so innovative in the Greek context that one of the problems experienced by Arsis has been prejudice and suspicion. However, another innovative element of Arsis' work involves continuous education and public relations work in order to gain support for its work.

Spain

The Coordinadora de Transseuntes de Zaragoza in Spain (*Case Study 23*, Appendix) is an umbrella organisation for five charities attempting coordinated action with Zaragoza Municipality to provide an integrated system of service delivery to a hitherto neglected section of the homeless population, namely those who slip through the net of existing provision, the chronically homeless. Coordinadora provides services for about 20 people at any one time. Teams of volunteers track down the chronically homeless on the streets of Zaragoza, compile a dossier on their life-styles and routines and offer them sheltered accommodation at La Casa Abierta – a 'no requirements' centre managed by the municipality. The Coordinadora initiative recognises that resettlement and reintegration are beyond most of the residents, many of whom are elderly. The focus is on more limited objectives: time discipline, the development of self-esteem and control over and regulation by the residents of their own lives.

These examples demonstrate that specialisation may be necessary to ensure that the needs of particular vulnerable groups are appropriately met. It may, on the other hand, also be necessary because some people exhibit challenging behaviour which is not adequately catered for by other service provision. The French case study may also suggest that specialisation is a necessary adjunct of reintegration strategies for some individuals if the cycle of recidivism or the 'revolving door' of institutional living is to be broken.

Organisational management

Service integration

It has been suggested in Chapter 4 that networks of inter-organisational contacts are a necessary infrastructure for the occurrence of innovative capacity in voluntary organisations. Where such contacts are only weakly developed then we may expect also that the ability to develop integrated services would be impaired. The evidence from the case studies indicates that in some countries considerable effort, by both government and the voluntary sector, has occurred to develop, at the strategic level, the infrastructure of coordination and contact necessary to sustain the integration of services. Evidence of such initiatives, for example, in Ireland, is described above in Chapter 5. However, there is also evidence of the integration of a range of services at the organisational level and these are described below.

Austria

In Austria the Wohnplattform (Housing Platform) Linz project (*Case Study 1*, Appendix) provides an example of an attempt to integrate housing provision with a range of support services. The project originated from an informal working group of social workers who had a common interest in resolving the difficulties of identifying and maintaining suitable housing for their clients. The group saw housing as an essential element in the effective delivery of their social services. With their common interests and aims, they established the Housing Platform, a membership organisation that provides transitory housing while each of the member agencies provides support to the clients referred to the project. In common with several other case studies, the origins of this project lie in the social work sphere rather than the housing sphere. Frequently, it is social services which is driving the recognition of the multi-faceted needs of vulnerable people and highlighting housing as a critical area of need. Membership agencies such as Housing Platform Linz are being created to respond to the identified housing needs of vulnerable people.

The Inigo project in Austria (*Case Study 2*, Appendix) is an example of an initiative directed at the integration of housing and employment, or at least of training for employment. Described as a 'socioeconomic enterprise' it provides training for 17 young people in all aspects of running a restaurant. Typically, young people are involved with the project for a period of eight months. Service users usually have a long history of exclusion from the labour market, which has also affected all aspects of their lives. The project aims to provide training and skill qualification through direct and profitable employment and works with social services agencies who provide social assistance programmes to meet individual needs.

Portugal

In Portugal, in a Lisbon-based project (*Case Study 21*, Appendix), the Municipality of Lisbon has cooperated with two non-profit organisations (the Foundation of International Medical Assistance, AMI, and the

Association of Christian Fraternity) to develop an integration programme, based on individual assistance and focusing primarily on work aimed at selecting individuals for on-the-job-training in civil construction. The AMI also offers an 'employment club' to assist the unemployed in finding work. This assistance involves information about job vacancies, training in one of the training centres supported by the Institute of Employment and Occupational Training and assistance with transport to work.

Spain

In Spain the San Martin de Porres project based in Madrid (*Case Study 22*, Appendix) provides shelter for 72 people with no limit on duration of stay. It collaborates with other organisations in developing a common strategy for dealing with the homeless in Madrid. Its aim is to implement service delivery for emergency and longer-term resettlement and to provide reintegration solutions, which explicitly involve employment. Residents who are showing an inclination to self-help in actively seeking employment are rewarded by being given access to all of the shelter's facilities; those that show no such inclination have more restricted access. The facilities include: an occupational workshop, a creative space for utilisation of resident's skills; professional training with six full-time employees in a binding workshop which caters for local customers and supplies external companies; integration services through which support workers provide job seeking advice and maintain contact after a job has been obtained; a form of outreach support and residential integration which provides assistance with flat finding and support follow-up. A mini-residence provides an intermediary position between the shelter and individually tenanted flats where independent living can be practised. It comprises communal flatted accommodation for 15 people who take some responsibility for rent payments and organisation of routines. Finally, there is a citizenship centre for newspaper reading, telephone calls and other everyday private activities.

The evidence from these case studies illustrate the issues involved in service integration in relation to both coordinating a range of services and to the integration of housing and employment. The examples quoted suggest that such innovation is characteristic of all the welfare and housing regimes described in Chapter 2.

Funding mechanisms and agency services

The institutional framework we are using for the analysis of service provision suggests that financial management is an important dimension at the organisational as well as the strategic level of analysis. Innovation in this latter context might involve the development of new funding mechanisms or the innovative application of existing financial sources. The development and management of services for homeless people will involve both capital and revenue funding.

We have already seen above how agency services such as the Y-Foundation in Finland and SWH in Germany have been used to facilitate the capital funding required for the development of new accommodation programmes. Examples of projects using new sources of capital finance have also been described earlier, including those in Germany, the Netherlands and Spain. These projects are generally described as having a limited life span and the implications of this are considered in Chapter 5. New financial sources may sometimes become available through targeted government initiatives, or for capital investment associated with new construction or redevelopment projects (for example, in the Rough Sleepers Initiative in Britain, or in projects associated with urban regeneration programmes in Germany).

However, experience would suggest that it is revenue funding, required for project management, which present the more persistent and difficult challenges for service providers, whether in the public or voluntary sector. The ongoing revenue funding needed to manage and develop homeless people's services is likely to involve the matching of finance from disparate sources over uncertain or different time-scales. There are a few examples cited in the case studies of the innovative use of revenue funding for service provision.

Austria

In Austria, the Inigo project in Vienna, as we have seen above, is a socioeconomic enterprise offering training and employment to young people through a restaurant business (*Case Study 2*, Appendix). The project receives partial funding from the Public Labour Office and the European Fund (48%). A further 5% of the costs are raised by Caritas, the organising agency. But the remaining 47% of funding is raised through the activities of its own restaurant activities. At a time when many restaurants in Vienna are experiencing financial decline, the continued growth of this particular restaurant is innovative in that it enables the project to gain financial independence from the constantly shrinking public purse.

Germany

In Germany, in the Soziale Wohnraumhilfe Hanover (SWH) project, capital costs of construction were covered by 52% state subsidies, 40% private finance and 8% church donations (*Case Study 12*, Appendix). Operating costs were met by a combination of land, municipal and church finance and the church also provided a risk guarantee fund for irrecoverable debts (for example, from rent arrears). In this way the accommodation costs for homeless people rehoused into normal housing were estimated to be little more than half of the costs of accommodation in a homeless institution. However, the revenue funding of social care proved more problematic. Initial prognoses by social workers of the nature and length of time for which support would be required for people being rehoused proved erroneous. Social care was financed for only a limited time and only half of the residents had claim to personal care provision by institutions from which they had been rehoused. SWH was able to step into such situations to protect residents from becoming homeless again. The conclusion to be drawn from this project is that the organisation, financing and quality of social care for rehoused homeless persons has to be improved considerably.

Italy

In Italy a 'new convention' has been drawn up between the local authority and the two main private housing and care associations, San Marcellino and Caritas, which defines a new type of relationship between the social services and these private organisations (*Case Study 17*, Appendix). This convention ensures a steady flow of public sector finance to the two associations and employs a Technical Operational Group to deal specifically with persons of no abode.

It can be argued that one of the aims of innovation in service provision is to improve the efficiency and effectiveness of the service. This will often be associated with the development of methods to improve the use of available resources of funding, professional expertise or accommodation. One aspect of innovation in this context is the development of 'primary–secondary' relationships between agencies to pool scarce resources and to facilitate the sharing of specialist expertise or resources between service providers. A number of examples of such innovation are apparent and these represent a particular form of coordination in the contact relationship between agencies. Our interpretation of the evidence of the origin and function of these relationships is that they may arise both as a result of endogenous factors, for example, the rationale to maintain the separation of housing and support functions, and also as a result of exogenous forces, for example, the need for economies of scale and speculums when operating in the private money markets. Finland and Germany provide examples of innovation in the provision of such 'agency services' or 'primary–secondary' relationships between agencies.

Finland

The history of the formation of the Y-Foundation in Finland has been described above. As a national umbrella organisation, one of the roles of the organisation is to work together with social welfare and healthcare authorities to estimate need in each municipality for supported accommodation. It also, in effect, acts as a property agency on behalf of other organisations acquiring accommodation in areas where the need is determined and agreement has been reached for the provision of the necessary support.

Germany

In a similar manner to the Finnish example, the German SWH agency provides a service to other organisations in the finance, administration and management of property required for supported accommodation projects.

At the organisational management level of analysis it becomes clear that while there is some innovation in the provision of capital finance for the construction of new dwellings, there is more difficulty in matching innovation in revenue funding. However, there is increasing evidence of the development of primary–secondary relationships between organisations to take advantage of the economies of scale which such organisational structures can involve.

Organisational implementation

Flexible and responsive services

The institutional framework of service provision employed in this study (Figure 4.3) suggests that the innovative capacity of organisations will be driven, in part, by the response to social need and by responsiveness to the client base (the end-user). This implies that an organisation must have the ability to adapt its 'products' to perceived needs and to be sensitive to the wishes of those to whom its services are aimed.

Our analysis of the governance context and social welfare models within which organisations in Europe are operating further suggests that voluntary organisations are increasingly operating in a culture predicated by a market ideology and in a situation of public expenditure restraint. Market models of procurement are manifest in the role of the public sector (and increasingly the municipal or lower executive tier of government) as purchasers of services provided by voluntary agencies which are mediated through mechanisms of performance management. This process, together with expenditure constraint, may lead to change and innovation in service delivery as a reaction to the competitive bidding processes which may be involved or to the restriction or uncertainty in the funding levels and performance assurance mechanisms adopted by the purchasing authorities. Our interpretation of the evidence suggests that the funding providers require evidence not only of output (the number of homeless people provided with services) but also of outcomes (the achievement of reintegration policy objectives) if public expenditure is to be justified.

Thus, at this organisational level of analysis, the implementation dimension would suggest that innovation may occur, perhaps as a reaction to exogenous forces described above as well as proactively because of changes in organisational values and goals, within organisations to establish structures and procedures which can respond to the performance management requirements of funding providers. It would also suggest that innovation might occur in the linkages or packaging of services to provide flexible solutions to a range of needs. In the remainder of this section we examine the evidence, from the case studies, of the situations where organisations' management structures have been adapting to take account of these pressures. The next section will examine the impact of these changes at the operational level insofar as they have led to change in the provision and operation of services and have involved users.

Examples of innovation within the structure and procedures of organisations include the following examples drawn from the case study evidence provided in the Appendix.

Italy

An innovative aspect of the San Marcellino project in Italy (*Case Study 17*, Appendix) is the recognition of the multi-dimensional nature of the problems of people of no-abode and the organisation of a series of diversified facilities for each of the five areas of potential hardship: housing, employment, relationships, addiction (alcohol and drugs) and illness (physical and mental). Flexibility and openness are key words in the organisational approach adopted by this project and thus the organisation of the centre is continuously changing; facilities are established and closed or transformed to match currently understood needs. The structure and management procedures of the organisation reflect this overall philosophy and involve a network approach in which there is coordination between the various sectors of the project and between the project and external agencies. Each section within the project is responsible for an annual review of its activities and reports to a Study Group, which constitutes a reference point for section activities on behalf of the Management Council.

United Kingdom

Wernham House in Aberdeen is a UK-based example of innovation in organisational implementation (*Case Study 26*, Appendix). Managed by Aberdeen Cyrenians, this is a wet hostel providing accommodation in a non-judgemental and non-punitive atmosphere for 18 men and women who have severe alcohol and/or mental health problems. The project addresses the multiple needs of a very marginalised population. There is no emphasis on traditional success measures, such as those of resettlement to a permanent tenancy. The aims are more modest and flexible: to remove residents from a spiral and cyclical round of institutionalisation while providing a supportive secure and safe environment for maximisation of independence and self-esteem. In this respect, the project challenges traditional notions of reintegration. The focus is on empowerment and acceptance of responsibility rather than on treatment and cure. Residents are encouraged to personalise their rooms; they choose their own linen and can decorate to their own taste; many have their own TV and can eat in their own rooms, though communal meals and a communal TV are provided. Residents can bring drink and friends into the hostel. When a resident wants resettlement every encouragement is given, but there is no pressure; a relaxed view is taken of the process and its desirability. Resettlement candidates are provided with a support worker from Aberdeen Cyrenian staff. Only six residents have moved on to tenancies of their own; all have been successful.

At this organisational level of analysis, innovation is observed in the provision of flexible services which include changes in the internal structures of organisations and in their external relationships or coordination. Responsive services are required which also recognise the difficulty of reintegrating some individuals and such projects aim to provide services which are responsive to user demands.

Conclusion

The reintegration of homeless and long-term homeless people into permanent affordable housing with normal tenancy rights has been an emerging and key organisational objective in the 1990s. There is some evidence from the case studies across Europe (for example, in Germany, Finland, Belgium and the Netherlands) that this can be successfully achieved even for people who have experienced long periods of institutional living and for people who have a low capacity for independent living. The development of supported housing has been a critical element of this success. The evidence here suggests that there is a wide variety of approaches to the provision and management of supported housing but that it may not be a suitable solution to reintegration in all situations. The importance of combining housing reintegration with labour market integration is most strongly highlighted in the case studies from countries in the continental and Mediterranean welfare regimes. However, the need for the integration of services is inherent in all countries where the understanding of the multi-dimensional nature of homelessness exists.

SEVEN

Services for the homeless: operational innovation

Introduction

To the extent that the principles underlying policies aimed at reintegration include empowerment and normalisation, there is an implication that services for the homeless, both in their content and in their method of delivery, should be responsive to the user's needs, should involve the user in shaping their content and delivery and should aspire to achieving user satisfaction or effecting change in the life circumstances of the individual. In this context 'clients' become 'participants' – service users with rights rather than simply welfare recipients.

The concept of empowerment involves users taking or being given more power over decisions affecting their welfare and hence involves some redistribution of power away from service and support providers (Means and Smith, 1994). Barnes and Walker (1996), in differentiating the concept of empowerment from a consumerist approach that they argue is still too centred on service provision, distinguish two polar forms of service organisation: bureaucratic and empowering (Figure 7.1). The principles of empowerment, Barnes and Walker argue, emphasise the rights of the individual rather than their role as a consumer of services.

Taking these principles as a guide, innovation at the operational level may be defined conceptually to involve an individualised approach to needs assessment, a negotiated contractual approach to service provision and a review of service provision in response to user outcomes. Such innovations would be manifest in operational planning, operational organisation and operational implementation (Figure 7.2).

Figure 7.1: Service organisation models

Bureaucratic	Empowering
Service/provider-oriented	User-oriented
Inflexible	Responsive
Provider-led	Needs-led
Power-concentrated	Power-sharing
Defensive	Open to review
Conservative	Open to change
Input-orientated	Outcome oriented

Source: Barnes and Walker (1996)

Figure 7.2: Operational innovation

	Planning	Management	Implementation
Operational level	• Effecting change for individuals • Levels of user satisfaction	• Care planning and management	• Needs assessment

Overall, the nature of development and change in service provision in the member states of the EU show a general trend towards a more individualised approach to service delivery. At the strategic planning level this is reflected in the trend towards small–scale accommodation provision. At the implementation level it is reflected in approaches which aim to match services to individual needs assessment. Specifically, the case studies illustrate the following types of innovation.

In operational planning:
• the development of contractual relationships between the service provider and the service user which defines objectives and outcomes; the introduction of independent review procedures to evaluate expectations and outcomes and identify required changes.

In operational management:
• the provision of flexibility and/or diversity in service delivery in response to changing user needs.

In operational implementation:
•   individual needs assessment and service plan.

Operational planning

Negotiated contractual approach

The principles of normalisation and empowerment are central to the concept of reintegration. These principles will be reflected, in practice, in different procedures and professional roles. The nature of the relationship between the service provider and the individual will be radically different to approaches based on traditional values of control and treatment. One response which is evident from the case studies and which defines this new relationship is in the form of individual contract or care plan that establishes the expectations and responsibilities of both parties to the contract.

Italy

In Italy the San Marcellino Association (*Case Study 17*, Appendix) has developed a programme for the social reinsertion of 'persons of no abode' using a variety of different resources and instruments. Very different types of accommodation have been made available with the aim of producing special purpose instruments to meet different needs. As it is currently organised, social workers work with users to reconstruct biographies, negotiate rehabilitation plans and reinterpret and review experiences in the various facilities which are available to meet needs. The starting point when responding to the needs of those with no abode is to establish a meaningful relationship and then negotiate with the participating client the steps to be taken. Such an approach is intended to ensure that the participating person takes ownership of their own rehabilitation plan.

Luxembourg

In Luxembourg people who are referred to the Wunnengshellef project (*Case Study 18*, Appendix) by its member agencies enter into a written contractual agreement. The contract details the personalised care and support plan which service users are obliged to accept. While the written contract itself is a step forward in terms of outlining rights and responsibilities, the extent to which the requirement to accept the support offered, and its potential link to the issue of security of tenure, may detract from the empowerment and normalisation of the service user is unclear.

The evidence from these case studies illustrates that the individualised approach to service delivery involves an element of negotiation in the assessment process. This is inevitable since the presenting problem is often not the key problem to be addressed if the objective of normalisation and reintegration is to be achieved; a long-term perspective will often need to focus on problems other than the immediate or crisis issues. It also confirms the conceptual view that normalisation implies that the individual must take ownership of the rehabilitation plan if it is to succeed. Hence the importance of a negotiated approach which may involve compromise by both parties to the agreement in the construction of an acceptable solution or plan.

Review of outcomes and services

Services can only be responsive to users' needs and be modified to improve user satisfaction if the organisation has feedback from the service users. The existence of monitoring mechanisms also presumes that the culture of the organisation is driven by the principles of reintegration discussed in Chapter 6. Mechanisms for monitoring and review can be expensive to implement in terms of staff time and it is to be expected that such innovations will take time to evolve. This may partly explain why there were few references in the case study material to formal mechanisms of monitoring and review (see Chapter 8).

Assessment of the internal work carried out at San Marcellino (*Case Study 17*, Appendix) occurs on two levels – assessment of individual cases and general assessment of the project's activities. The latter (see the Operational implementation section in Chapter 6), involves a yearly sector-by-sector review when the Centre closes for a week and the manager and volunteers of each sector carry out a review and verification of its activities and reports to a Study Group, which in turn acts as a consultancy body for the Management Council. Assessment of individual cases is firstly undertaken by the social worker but since there is no standard casework plan, there is no standard measure valid for all.

This example illustrates some important aspects of monitoring. First, a review of outcomes requires procedures and systems within the organisational structure of the agency and implies that staff are trained and share the understanding of the importance and purpose of review. Second, it implies that service specification and objectives are clear and provide targets or benchmarks against which outcomes can be judged. Finally, the decision-making structures of the organisation need to be able to respond appropriately and timeously to the monitoring information. The example here also illustrates that there may be conceptual difficulties in establishing measures of success in relation to individual outcomes. These difficulties arise from the relative nature of individual needs and from the often long-term and cyclical time periods involved.

Operational management

Flexibility in service provision

An important principle guiding service provision is the recognition of the multi-faceted nature of the causes of homelessness and therefore of the needs of individual homeless people. Appropriate responses to this involve not only the integration of services but also the ability to respond flexibly to changes in the user's circumstances or needs. It is to be expected that people who have experienced lengthy periods of institutional living or who have led chaotic life-styles will initially require a high level of support to facilitate their transition to independent living. It is also evident that people who have a mental illness or have drug or alcohol problems have needs which may fluctuate from requiring very high levels of support to periods involving lower levels of dependency. There is some debate about the accuracy of conceptualising such situations as a 'continuum of care' needs and therefore of the efficacy of tailoring services on this basis. Nevertheless, there are a number of examples of attempts to provide a diversity of linked services to enable people to move up or down this 'ladder (or staircase) of care'.

Netherlands

In the Netherlands, Walenburg is an example of a 'step-model' project in Amsterdam, which aims to offer a complete range of possibilities from a permanent shelter for older men via accommodation that is adjacent to the shelter, to independent housing with visiting support and, as a final step, to independent living (*Case Study 20*, Appendix). The step-model is described as a means by which inhabitants can climb up the ladder depending on their capacities, but in case of problems can always fall back to an earlier phase if they require more support. Step One is described as a shelter for homeless men with a capacity of 60 beds. Step Two is a shelter in which clients have their own apartments (including toilets and showers) and share common rooms and where meals are provided. Step Three consists of 37 small apartments in two buildings where people live on their own, but still get their meals from the central shelter. Step Four involves residents preparing their own meals and receiving as little support as possible; at this stage apartments are spread all over the city. Throughout these steps the resident is a client rather than a tenant, which is to say that he has a boarding agreement rather than a tenancy agreement and is therefore dependent on the shelter, which can end the agreement if the client does not conform to the rules.

Sweden

The Swedish 'Staircase of Transition' (*Case Study 24*, Appendix) is designed to reintegrate homeless people into the regular housing market. Though not a model imposed on or even recommended to the municipalities, as the staircase emerged and spread, central government adjusted legislation to accommodate its development. Progress up the staircase is characterised by an incremental increase in housing standards, security and responsibilities and a cumulatively progressive decline in the provision of support and services. The final step is achieved when a tenant gets their own leasehold flat or house. The time spent at different levels on the staircase varies, but there is an assumption that it will take a few years to climb the entire staircase. Characteristically, local social authorities rent the homes from housing associations or from private landlords and sub-lease the property to clients on special terms. Most local authorities have put in place some version of the staircase and, while larger municipalities often have larger projects, the size of projects also reflects variations in municipal policies. Local variations may mean that different localities have differently constructed staircases with the number and type of steps demonstrating some variation and locally specific characteristics. An ideal typical model, however, can be described as having three steps: *category houses* – small flats, often of low standard, provided as group homes; *training flats* – sometimes ordinary dwellings, furnished and located near institutions with residents sometimes monitored by staff in a neighbouring institution; *transitional flats* – these are spread out in ordinary residential areas and tenants are responsible for their own furniture. While each step has a specific target group – older single men with alcohol problems and/or mental problems in category houses; people who have successfully participated in treatment programmes for substance abuse in training houses; and families with children who had been evicted or rejected because of debts or rent arrears in *transitional housing* – they are not exclusive to these groups; there is flexibility and no step excludes any group.

These case studies from the Netherlands and Sweden illustrate that there is still some reason for concern about the efficacy of the 'continuum of care' approach to service delivery. First, it is not certain that people's problems respond to the continuum approach of progressively lower levels of support leading to normal tenancies without support and hence full reintegration. Individual problems simply do not respond to such a prescriptive approach. Second, the steps on the ladder are difficult to construct to meet the diversity of needs encountered. Third, the integration involved in such a solution implies a close network of contacts between agencies involved in the ladder and a sophisticated procedure of assessment and referral. Finally, what effect does climbing down the ladder have on an individual's motivation to succeed? While insufficient evidence is given in the case studies, it is likely that such approaches are expensive in staff resources and require a high degree of coordination and staff training to operate effectively. Therefore the experience described in the case studies provides evidence for caution in the adoption of this particular form of innovation in service provision. The evidence from these examples also suggests (as we might expect) that the approach to flexible services involves taking advantage of the increasing diversity in service provision rather than actual flexibility by tailoring services, in a bespoke manner, to meet individual needs.

Operational implementation

The individualised approach

Traditional approaches to service provision, based on curative or palliative philosophies, have tended to be supply-led and to be based on a normative and prescriptive definition of need. Services whose aim is reintegration require, by definition, to be focused on an individualised assessment of need and, as described above, to be responsive and flexible in designing solutions to meet the assessed needs. The move towards an individualised approach to service provision is common wherever the reintegration philosophy is embraced and therefore many of the case studies include examples of this approach or describe the move in this direction (the Italian example has already been described above, *Case Study 17*). The following examples typify this approach.

France

At La Roche sur Yon in France, a network of existing and diverse services for homeless people has been developed (*Case Study 9*, Appendix). While the members of the network work together to develop a common understanding and awareness of the needs of and services for homeless people in the area, there is no attempt at a fully integrated response. Instead, the diversity, complexity and individuality of the service user's choice are respected and several different but networked options are offered. The decision on the actual path taken is then left up to the individual. Commonly, when we speak of individualised approaches to service provision, what we mean is an individualised assessment and service delivery based on the individual's needs. While needs-led, this approach is also constrained by the parameters of the service provider's operational and organisational framework. The network approach at La Roche sur Yon seeks to break away from this model and opts instead to leave the choice of the type of service used up to the individual according to their own assessment of their needs and preferences. The different members of the network provide guidance and advice as well as information in making those choices.

Germany

The project in Bielefeld, Germany (*Case Study 13*, Appendix) provides an example of the trend to reduce the number of places at larger institutionalised shelters, incorporating a separation of accommodation and support or care, and an individualised approach to assessment, allocation and post-placement support. The reduction in places at the traditional shelter represents a substantial financial saving for the responsible authorities. This has enabled an agreement that guaranteed funding for a five-year period for requisite support provided on an individual basis for residents who have been reallocated from the shelter to the supported housing.

Portugal

Although the municipality leads the Lisbon project (*Case Study 21*, Appendix), it involves a number of other agencies, which means that the project is open to the variety of inputs that each client may need. The individualised approach is an important feature of the project to utilise the various services coordinated by the central agency (AMI). The individualised approach, which has been adopted, has implications for the maximum capacity of the project (25 men) and for the age cohort targeted (18- to 65-year-old men).

The individualised approach can only occur effectively if innovation has already occurred at the strategic and organisational levels of innovation. On the one hand, it requires, at the strategic level, a movement towards smaller-scale and homely living environments with appropriate levels of care. On the other hand, at the organisational level, the individualised approach requires adequate staff training and staffing levels and a culture which accepts the shift in the power relationship involved from the professional to the client. It also requires effective coordination between agencies at both the strategic and organisational levels involving planning of service provision, finance and service flexibility and delivery. Indeed, if we refer to our conceptual model of organisational framework (Chapter 4), the individualised approach requires an effective network of organisational contacts to operate effectively. Where such networks are underdeveloped, then it is unlikely that such innovation will occur or be successful.

Conclusion

Our interpretation of the evidence presented in the case studies suggests that empowerment is achieved, in the main, by the ability to match users' needs to a widening diversity of pre-existing services rather than the ability to offer bespoke services. On the other hand, there are a number of examples of individual needs assessment leading to negotiated contracts between the service provider and the service user. The evidence as presented is inconclusive in relation to the extent to which empowerment, as defined in the Barnes and Walker model (1996), is achieved and indeed there is an indication of a punitive element written into contracts for failure to comply. This may be understandable in relation to the challenging behaviour or chaotic life-styles of some service users but it does not indicate a redistribution of power away from the service or support provider to the extent implied by the concept of empowerment. Overall there is only limited evidence of the review of services in relation to outcomes which articulates the user's perspective. While the practical difficulties involved in this have to be recognised, there is little evidence of the organisational mechanisms (organisational objectives, structures and procedures and staff training) which are necessary for its implementation.

EIGHT

Conclusion

A significant feature of homelessness throughout Europe over the past 25 years has been its persistence. Traditional policies, largely derived and shaped in the immediate post-war decades, have increasingly been found wanting in the changed economic and demographic circumstances of the last quarter of the 20th century. A reappraisal of the nature of European homelessness, by both academics and practitioners, demonstrates the need for the development of innovatory policies and practices which take account of these changed circumstances in explicitly addressing the current needs of Europe's homeless people.

Our evaluation of innovation and change in service delivery to the homeless is premised on the notion that much of the incentive for innovation can be traced to the processes of economic restructuring and sociodemographic change in Europe in the past few decades. These processes have offered a challenge to the manner in which welfare and housing services have traditionally been delivered and have provided the catalyst for rethinking and reformulation. Drawing on the national reports of the 15 correspondents of the European Observatory on Homelessness (see Appendix), the first part of this report (Chapters 1, 2 and 3) charts the main dimensions of the reappraisal of the nature of homelessness, of its causes, of the composition of homeless populations and of policy instruments. These chapters provide a context for the second part of the report (Chapters 4, 5, 6 and 7) in which we examine in some detail the nature and diversity of emerging innovative practices in the provision of services to the homeless of Europe.

Reformulations of our understanding of the dimensions of European homelessness tend now, at the end of the century, to focus on their complexity and multi-faceted nature as exemplified in the diverse composition of the homeless population and in the multiple and varied causes of homelessness. Solutions to the problems of homelessness are now understood to require more than the provision of shelter; complex causes require complex solutions which focus as much on the acquisition of life skills as on the provision of a home. Such reformulations are embedded in a changing conception of the problem of homelessness, which has shifted the emphasis from a focus on pathology to a focus on societal issues. In this respect the notion of social exclusion has proved to be a useful vehicle for carrying forward our understanding of homelessness and for the derivation of innovative service practices which address the issues of integration and reintegration of homeless people into the mainstream of society. The best such practices also recognise that successful reintegration requires the eschewing of universalistic solutions in favour of programmes tailored to the specific needs of homeless individuals.

To the extent that the above reformulations have been accepted and adopted by European governments and by agencies responsible for the homeless, we might expect a European-wide emergence of a shared view of the nature of the problems faced by homeless people as well as a similarity in approach in the delivery of services designed to provide a solution to those problems. Indeed, such commonalities can be identified, for example, in a growing sensitivity to the complexity of the problem, in a recognition of the need for individualised solutions and in the orientation of services towards the target of integration. In addition commonalities can be distinguished in the manner of service delivery. In all European countries a convergence of housing policy is manifest in housing production and rehabilitation, in housing finance and subsidy, in the role of privatisation and in the changed nature of public sector responsibility (Kleinman et al, 1998). In particular, there is a near universal 'rolling back of the state': the withdrawal of the state from direct engagement with housing provision and its adoption of an enabling and regulatory role. In service delivery to the homeless, such changes are to be seen in the implementation of public–private partnerships, which replace state-funded and state-run organisations, and in the increased role of the voluntary sector as a critical medium for the delivery of services.

Yet within these broad commonalities, a striking diversity of approach can also be discerned. A diversity reflected, for example, in the degree and scale of innovation, in the extent to which traditional policies – or the absence of policies – have been replaced by new initiatives and in the extent to which policies of containment and compliance have been replaced by those which emphasise integration and empowerment. Such diversity, we argue, reflects the different welfare histories of the member states of the EU; different traditions of welfare and housing provision which are, in part at least, encapsulated in the notion of welfare and housing regimes (see Chapter 2).

Our argument is that there is a complex interrelationship between policy responses, social and economic change and institutional structures which, if it can be disentangled, can account for both the common trends and the diversity evident in the innovation in homelessness services. In the second part of our report, using an institutional framework for analysis, we have attempted to tease out some of these complex associations through a detailed examination of the strategic (coordination and national/regional policy initiatives), the organisational (defining targets and new project initiatives) and the operational (service delivery, user involvement) components of innovative service delivery to the homeless.

Innovation at the strategic level

Analysis of the nature and causes of innovation at the strategic level enables us to identify important interactions between national welfare and housing policies and changes in responses to the provision of services for the homeless. It allows an understanding to emerge of the changing perception of homelessness and its relation to issues of marginalisation and social exclusion by reference to the changing objectives of service provision.

It has been a feature of policy in some countries to develop pilot programmes specifically to encourage and stimulate innovation. These approaches appear to be more evident in northern European countries: France, Germany, the Netherlands and the UK are all cited in this respect. The programmes come from different policy derivations which include urban regeneration (Germany), street homelessness (UK) and social welfare (the Netherlands). However, on the basis of the evidence presented in the national reports, the significance of these innovations in leading to long-term shifts in approach to service delivery has proved difficult to assess, as has their effectiveness in providing new and cost-effective solutions which can be implemented within existing organisational structures and public expenditure regimes. While some of these programmes include funding for monitoring and evaluation, it is unlikely that such monitoring and evaluation will extend to assessing their effect on existing agencies and provision arising from the redirection of resource allocation.

One of the features of policy change and shifting political ideology in recent years has been a move towards market liberalisation and away from government intervention (Hutton, 1995). In the public sector this has been evident in the emergence of quasi-markets leading to competitive bidding and purchaser–provider funding mechanisms (Le Grand, 1993). The emergence of umbrella organisations, partnerships and new agencies is a rational and healthy response to such changes. However, this form of innovation may also be indicative of important, but questionable, changes in the institutional structures of service provision for the homeless. The need to compete for limited resources and to sustain quality services encourages the emergence of larger agencies, which are often driven as much by organisational goals as by service level objectives. Further, the reliance on scarce public sector funding, seeking safe and accountable investment, in an increasingly pluralistic market (as responsibility is decentralised to municipal authorities) could operate to stifle innovation and flexibility.

Our analysis has indicated that in some countries (the Netherlands, Denmark, and Belgium) new legislation has had a direct impact in encouraging innovation in service provision. For example, the introduction of legislation related to community care has led to the development of supported housing projects for the reintegration of homeless people, or those at risk of homelessness, into the community. However, many legislative initiatives have involved mainly social welfare policies rather than housing policies. It would require more detailed research than that conducted in this report to understand how well 'joined-up' are policies and procedures in relation to housing provision and social service delivery.

Elsewhere in this report (Chapter 2) we have described the social welfare systems in the Mediterranean countries as formative. There is some evidence to suggest that the state is beginning to accept responsibility for homelessness in these regions. The development of services, albeit of a more traditional emergency nature, can be seen as a welcome innovation in this context since it is indicative of state and municipal involvement, for the first time, in the provision of services to the homeless. However, such innovation appears, for the moment at least, to be localised rather than national in focus and to be predominantly urban-based.

While we remain cautious in ascribing specific forms of innovation or policy approach to specific housing regimes (for reasons rehearsed in Chapter 2), it does appear that strategic policy developments involving reintegration are more typically a feature of the Continental and Nordic countries rather than the Anglo-Saxon or Mediterranean countries.

Innovation at the organisational level

An important common trend across all European states is the role of non-governmental organisations (voluntary organisations or NGOs) in the provision of services for the homeless. This is a feature of countries in all housing regimes.

The reintegration of homeless and long-term homeless people into permanent affordable housing with normal tenancy rights raises a number of important issues at the organisational level. The case studies demonstrate that reintegration strategies, by their very nature, involve coordination between housing and social services as well as between the public sector (for example, in relation to community care planning) and voluntary service providers. It also involves homelessness organisations working with private and social landlords in a manner which will enable people at risk of homelessness to sustain a normal tenancy. Voluntary organisations can thus have a critical lead role in initiating supported housing projects, as well as in their management and implementation, often within the context of uncertain (short-term) funding regimes.

The need for service provision to respond to the multi-dimensional facets of the problems of homeless people has been stressed throughout our analysis. The implications of such an approach (which are discussed in Chapter 7) involve the need for flexibility and for an individualised approach to service provision. Such an approach also involves the integration of housing services with employment initiatives and welfare services. The successful introduction of more flexible and individualised approaches and the accommodation of the philosophy of service delivery that such approaches embrace, requires change to organisational structures and organisational procedures. Such organisational changes might include the introduction of more formalised structures for voluntary organisations including procedures for monitoring and review, changes in staffing levels and staff skills, and a greater emphasis on staff development.

The evidence from the case studies examined in this report suggests that where flexible packages of provision are offered, they are provided through coordination between existing agencies as well as by agencies taking on new roles and adopting innovative procedures of service implementation. Both approaches have implications for the links between housing and social services, for the funding of these new forms of service delivery and for strategies for the development of service provision.

There is evidence, in some case studies (for example, those from Italy and France) of attempts to develop mechanisms of review and evaluation that will allow agencies to learn, adapt and be responsive to changing user requirements or to new and emerging needs. However, such evaluation of new initiatives is not commonly or consistently undertaken. It appears that formal mechanisms of review and monitoring are still in their infancy in most NGOs, and that there is much to be shared and learnt from those organisations that have pioneered such developments.

Innovation at the operational level

We have argued in the body of our report that the principles of normalisation and empowerment are central to the concept of reintegration. Approaches to the solution of homelessness which focus on prevention and reintegration will therefore require a different orientation to the values which have underlain the more traditional responses of control and treatment. In particular, a more individualised care management or planning approach is predicated. This in turn implies a greater flexibility in services and a willingness and ability to tailor services to meet a range of individualised needs. It also implies the ability to assess outcomes as well as outputs (that is to say, improvements in individual quality of life and not simply measurement of the numbers of people provided with a particular service).

In effect, such an approach to reintegration involves the creation of a customer contract outlining the roles and responsibilities of each party to the contract and guaranteeing the rights of the recipient (that is to say, the approach is rooted in a citizenship model of welfare). It is perhaps to be anticipated that only a small number of examples of such approaches are cited in this report since this is the emerging challenge facing providers of services to the homeless as we approach the *fin de siècle*.

The case studies examined here illustrate the difficulties involved in offering flexible services to people whose support needs and levels of dependency may fluctuate over time. The analysis of such services also sounds a strong note of caution against conceptualising such situations as a 'continuum of care' and questions the efficacy of providing services on this basis.

The move towards a more individualised approach to service provision is reported in many of the case studies analysed in this study. Our conclusion regarding the implementation of such an approach to service delivery is that it requires an effective network of organisational contacts and cooperation to operate effectively. We also conclude that it implies that innovation has already occurred at the strategic level (for example, in creating small-scale living environments) and at the organisational level (for example, in changing organisational goals and procedures). There is room for concern, however, especially where such innovation accompanies service reprovisioning following institutional closure, that the funding commitment of public sector agencies to such initiatives tends to be relatively short-term and is frequently time-limited.

Conclusions and future research

This report has identified some interesting and exciting innovations in service delivery to the homeless. It has been an ambitious project and inevitably there has been some slippage in drawing out the full nature of the linkages and connections between the component parts and in identifying the full significance of these innovations in the fight against homelessness. We would suggest that in terms of further study three topics in particular could be identified for investigation.

At the most general level, there are questions that relate to issues of *convergence and divergence*. In an increasingly integrated Europe the conditions would seem to be conducive to the increasing convergence of economic and social structures and political organisations. We might therefore expect, as this integration proceeds, a diminished diversity in the way housing issues are dealt with across Europe, a coming together of policy and practice. Yet such convergence is by no means certain given the historically determined and deep-seated variety of social, political, economic and cultural conditions across European countries. In addition, with the anticipated expansion of the EU to incorporate some East European countries the existing diversity, for example, that between North and South, is scheduled to be reinforced by an East–West diversity. What is the future of housing policy and provision for the homeless in such circumstances? Kleinman et al's recent work (1998) hints at some of these issues in relation to housing policy generally – there is a need to expand such considerations to explicitly incorporate the issue of homelessness. In particular we would suggest that there is a need, as Europe moves towards greater harmonisation of welfare policies, to examine the real costs of housing exclusion and how these impact in different countries of the Union.

The second area of investigation that we would wish to highlight relates to a topic identified earlier in this concluding chapter, namely *monitoring and evaluation*. Some of the innovations reported on in this study are reasonably well established while others have only just come on stream. In all cases, however, there is a clear need to engage in an evaluative assessment of the success or otherwise of these projects. Such an assessment is a necessary preliminary to determining whether these innovations are worthy of replication within their country of origin and whether they are transferable across national boundaries. Such assessment, however, may be problematic unless clear assessment criteria can be established. Concepts such as integration and empowerment, for example, are difficult to measure with precision not least because judgement on the basis of these criteria are subject both to time delays and to potential distortion by vested interests. Equally, it is evident that transnational comparisons would require, at the European level, the adoption of consistent operational definitions and methods of data collection. Research in this area would have to deal with these difficult and vexed questions.

The third area of investigation, which we feel has been highlighted by the results of this report on innovative services, is the *relationship between housing provision and support provision*. The most innovative schemes addressed in this report, the ones which seem most likely to have an impact on preventing homelessness and have clear prospects of achieving the stated goal of reintegration, are small-scale projects designed to provide support packages tailored to individual needs. Supported housing is the provision of housing with support which aims to prevent and cure homelessness by enabling those people who have difficulty managing in mainstream housing to sustain tenancies and live independently. This issue is considered in the next stage of the research programme of the European Observatory on Homelessness and will be the subject of the next Observatory report.

References

Abernethy, W., Clark, K. and Kantrow, A. (1983) *Industrial renaissance*, New York, NY: Basic Books.

Abrahamson, P. (1992) 'Welfare pluralism: towards a new consensus for a European Social Policy?', in L. Hantrais, S. Mangen and M. O'Brien (eds) *The mixed economy of welfare*, Loughborough: Cross-National Research Papers, Loughborough University.

Aldridge, R. (1998) *National report 1997: United Kingdom*, Brussels: FEANTSA.

Allen, J. (1998) 'Europe of the neighbourhoods: class, citizenship and welfare regimes', in A. Madanipour, G. Cars and J. Allen (eds) *Social exclusion in European cities: Processes, experiences and responses*, London: Jessica Kingsley, pp 25-51.

Avramov, D. (1995) *Homelessness in the European Union. Social and legal context of housing exclusion in the 1990s*, Brussels: FEANTSA.

Avramov, D. (1996a) *Exclusion from housing: causes and processes*, Brussels: FEANTSA.

Avramov, D. (1996b) 'Data sources on homelessness and data necessary for a needs-based research project', Paper presented at the EUROHOME project Workshop 1: Data on Homelessness, Brussels: FEANTSA.

Avramov, D. (1998) *Youth homelessness in Europe*, Brussels: FEANTSA.

Balchin, P. (1996) *Housing policy in Europe*, London: Routledge.

Barlow, J. and Duncan, S. (1994) *Success and failure in housing provision*, London: Pergamon.

Barnes, M. and Walker, A. (1996) 'Consumerism versus empowerment: a principled approach to the involvement of older service users', *Policy & Politics*, vol 24, no 4, pp 375-93.

Børner Stax, T. (with I. Koch-Nielson) (1998) *National report 1997: Denmark*, Brussels: FEANTSA.

Bruto da Costa, A. (1998) *National report 1997: Portugal*, Brussels: FEANTSA.

Busch-Geertsema, V. (1998) *National report 1997: Germany*, Brussels: FEANTSA.

Cousins, C. (1998) 'Social exclusion in Europe: paradigms of social disadvantage in Germany, Spain, Sweden and the United Kingdom', *Policy & Politics*, vol 26, no 2, pp 127-46.

Cousins, M. (1998) 'Ireland's place in the world of welfare capitalism', *Journal of European Social Policy*, vol 7, no 3, pp 223-35.

Daly, M. (1999) 'Regimes of social policy in Europe and the patterning of homelessness', in D. Avramov (ed) *Coping with homelessness: Problems to be tackled and best practices*, Aldershot: Ashgate, pp 309-30.

de Decker, P. (1998) *National report 1997: Belgium*, Brussels: FEANTSA.

de Feijter, H. (1998) *National report 1997: Netherlands*, Brussels: FEANTSA.

de Gouy, A. (1998) *National report 1997: France*, Brussels: FEANTSA.

Donzelot, J. (ed) (1991) *Face á l'exclusion. La modèle français*, Paris: Editions Esprit.

Esping-Andersen, G. (1990) *The three worlds of welfare capitalism*, Cambridge: Polity Press.

FEANTSA (Fédération Européenne D'Associations Nationales Travaillant avec les Sans-Abri) (1995) *Is the European Union housing its poor?*, Brussels: FEANTSA.

FEANTSA (1999) *Europe against exclusion: Housing for all*, London: FEANTSA and Shelter.

Ferrera, M. (1996) 'The "southern model" of welfare in social Europe', *Journal of European Social Policy*, vol 6, no 1, pp 17-37.

Foucault, M. (1979) *Discipline and punishment*, New York, NT: Vintage Books.

Freitas, M.J.L. (1998) 'Mobilising community resources in Portugal', in A. Madanipour, G. Cars and J. Allen (eds) *Social exclusion in European cities*, London: Jessica Kingsley, pp 211-34.

George, V. and Taylor-Gooby, P. (eds) (1996) *European welfare policy: Squaring the circle*, London: Sage Publications.

Giddens, A. (1979) *Central problems in social theory*, London: Macmillan.

Giddens, A. (1984) *The constitution of society*, Cambridge: Polity Press.

Greve, J. (1986) *Homelessness in London*, Working Paper 60, Bristol: SAUS Publications.

Hall, S. and Jacques, M. (1989) *New times: The changing face of politics in the 1990s*, London: Lawrence and Wishart.

Harloe, M. (1995) *The people's home? Social rented housing in Europe and America*, Oxford: Blackwell.

Hutton, W. (1995) *The state we're in*, London: Routledge.

Johnson, B., Murie, A., Naumann, L. and Yanetta, A. (1991) *A typology of homelessness*, Edinburgh: Scottish Homes.

Kärkkäinen, S.L. and Hassi, L. (1998) *National report 1979: Finland*, Brussels: FEANTSA.

Kemeny, J. (1995) *Housing and social theory*, London: Routledge.

Kemeny, J. and Lowe, S. (1998) 'Schools of comparative housing research: from convergence to divergence', *Housing Studies*, vol 13, no 2, pp 161-76.

Kleinman, M. (1996) *Housing, welfare and the state in Europe: A comparative analysis of Britain, France and Germany*, Cheltenham: Edward Elgar.

Kleinman, M.P., Matznetter, W. and Stephens, M. (1998) *European integration and housing policy*, London: Routledge.

Kofler, A. (1998) *National report 1997: Austria*, Brussels: FEANTSA.

Leal Maldonado, J. and Lainez Romano, T. (1998) *National report 1997: Spain*, Brussels: FEANTSA.

Le Grand, J. (1993) *Quasi-markets and community care*, Bristol: SAUS Publications.

Madanipour, A. (1998) 'Social exclusion and space', in A. Madanipour, G. Cars and J. Allen (eds) *Social exclusion in European cities: Processes, experiences and responses*, London: Jessica Kingsley, pp 75-94.

Means, R. and Smith, R. (1994) *Community care: Policy and practice*, Basingstoke: Macmillan.

Mishra, R. (1990) *The welfare state in capitalist society*, London: Harvester Wheatsheaf.

Neale, J. (1997) 'Homelessness and theory reconsidered', *Housing Studies*, vol 12, no 1, pp 47-62.

O'Sullivan, E. (1998) *National report 1997: Ireland*, Brussels: FEANTSA.

Osborne, S. P. (1998) 'The innovative capacity of voluntary organisations: managerial challenges for local government', *Local Government Studies*, vol 21, no 1, pp 19-40.

Pels, M. (1998) *National report 1997: Luxembourg*, Brussels: FEANTSA.

Pinch, S. (1997) *Worlds of welfare: Understanding the changing geographies of social welfare provision*, London: Routledge.

Room, G. (ed) (1995) *Beyond the threshold: The measurement and analysis of social exclusion*, Bristol: The Policy Press.

Rowley, D. (ed) (1995) (CC2) *Planning, managing and implementing community care*, Dundee: Social Work Department, University of Dundee.

Sainsbury, D. (1992) *Gendering welfare states*, London: Sage Publications.

Sapounakis, A. (1998) *National report 1997: Greece*, Brussels: FEANTSA.

Sahlin, I. (1998) *National report 1997: Sweden*, Brussels: FEANTSA.

Silver, H. (1994) 'Social exclusion and social solidarity: three paradigms', *International Labour Review*, vol 133, no 56, pp 531-78.

Silver, H. (1997) 'Culture, politics and national discourses of the new urban poverty', in E. Mingione (ed) *Urban poverty and the underclass: A reader*, Oxford: Blackwell, pp 105-38.

Tosi, A. (1997a) 'Homelessness and the housing factor: learning from the debate on homelessness and poverty', Paper presented at EUROHOME project, Workshop 3: 'Risks of Homelessness', Brussels: FEANTSA.

Tosi, A. (1997b) 'The excluded and the homeless: the social construction of the fight against poverty in Europe', in A. Mingione (ed) *Urban poverty and the underclass: A reader*, Oxford: Blackwell, pp 83-104.

Tosi, A. (1998) *National report 1997: Italy*, Brussels: FEANTSA.

Vranken, J. (1997) 'Different policy approaches to homelessness', Paper presented at EUROHOME project, Workshop 3: 'Risks of Homelessness', Brussels: FEANTSA.

Watson, S. (1984) 'Definitions of homelessness: a feminist perspective', *Critical Social Policy*, no 11, pp 60–73.

Watson, S. and Austerberry, H. (1986) *Housing and homelessness: A feminist perspective*, London: Routledge.

Appendix: National case study summaries

Case study

Case study 1

Country:	Austria
Name of project:	*Wohnplattform Linz* (Housing Platform Linz)
Location:	Linz
Start date:	1984

Overview

The project has its origins in an informal working group of social workers employed by various regional institutions. The social workers were motivated by their common interest in resolving the difficulties of identifying and maintaining housing for their social work clients. A collaborative and cooperative interagency network was created to pool resources and reduce competition. Access to housing was seen as an essential ingredient in the effective delivery of social services.

The project provides transitional accommodation with support services to homeless people with a wide range of problems. Housing and support are delivered separately although provider agencies work cooperatively.

Aims and objectives

The aims of the project are:
• to coordinate and cooperate in the identification and allocation of appropriate housing;
• to raise public and political awareness of housing issues.

The objectives of the project are to rent, administer and maintain affordable housing for social work clients.

Innovation

The project is considered innovative because it aims to coordinate work and to operate in a cooperative spirit. This is a departure from the more common competitive and uncoordinated methods of working within both social services and housing.

Inputs

1 Agencies and partnerships

Wohnplattform Linz is a membership organisation involving a wide range of agencies. These include:

- women's shelters (domestic violence)
- advice, information and counselling services
- labour reintegration projects
- probation assistance for in and out of court work
- services for post-psychiatric care patients
- services for AIDS sufferers
- debt counselling services
- services for social reintegration with wide-ranging client groups
- legal services for the mentally ill.

In addition, affiliated members cooperate with the project on an informal basis.

The Upper Austrian Law relating to housing forms the legal basis for interagency cooperation. The legislation provides for preferential treatment of social services providers in obtaining leases for rental properties.

2 Areas and responsibility

Wohnplattform Linz provides the accommodation and is responsible for all aspects of housing management. The referring agencies who are members of *Wohnplattform Linz* provide the required support services on an individualised basis.

3 Target groups and numbers

Homeless people and people at risk of homelessness are the principal target groups. Referrals are made through member associations. There is a gender mix within the accommodation. The project is open to men, women and children (single people or families). In 1996, 50 men, 23 women and 24 children stayed in the accommodation.

4 Funding

Wohnplattform Linz is publicly funded, with 50% of costs paid by the City of Linz and 50% paid by the federal state of Upper Austria. There are two full-time and two part-time employees.

Implementation

I Services and delivery

Wohnplattform Linz provides transitory housing to people in need who are referred by member agencies. The umbrella organisation undertakes all housing management responsibilities. The usual maximum length of stay is one year and a large proportion of clients are able to access permanent housing within that time period. Social integration and support work is provided by the referring member agency on an individualised basis.

2 Accommodation

The accommodation includes both self-contained flats and shared housing. The project provides 63 apartments.

3 Integration

Integration is made possible through a stable home environment (as opposed to emergency housing) and the provision of social and labour market reinsertion programmes by social workers attached to the various member agencies. Reintegration programmes vary according to client group and individual needs.

Outputs

I Monitoring and evaluation

Unknown.

2 Problem areas

The attitude of financing agencies towards services for the homeless has been identified as one of the problem areas. These attitudes appear to be based on preconceptions and a continued perception that such services are primarily asylums. The result is underfunding of services for homeless people. Other problem areas include: the restrictive allocation procedures by public housing authorities; the lack of preventative and post-crisis intervention (outreach work); and the low quality of available affordable housing.

3 Dissemination

Unknown.

Case study 2

Country:	Austria
Name of project:	*Inigo*
Location:	Vienna
Start date:	Not known

Overview

This project is a socioeconomic enterprise offering employment/training in a protected environment to people with a long history of exclusion from the labour market. The project is not a direct provider of accommodation.

Aims and objectives

The aims of the project are:
- to offer employment to people traditionally excluded from the labour market;
- to provide an opportunity for skill and qualification development in a protected environment;
- to provide individualised social assistance programmes.

Innovation

Part of the project's innovation is its ability to gain independence from the constantly shrinking public funding purse. The project's success, both in terms of its own financial security and in terms of achieving its aims of reintegration in the labour market, is also innovative.

Inputs

1 Agencies and partnerships

The project is run by the Association of Social Facilities, an arm of Caritas. The project relies on other services for referral of suitable clients. It cooperates with the Public Labour Office, a variety of social service agencies and other enterprises within Caritas. The referral route through the Public Labour Office (*Arbeitsmarktservice* – *AMS*) is somewhat ineffective due to the lack of coordination and mutual understanding of the work of the project.

2 Areas and responsibility

Project staff include four restaurant experts, one social worker and a socioeconomic director.

3 Target groups and numbers

The project offers employment to 17 individuals. The project is open to people who have a history of long-term unemployment and those who suffer from particular discrimination in the labour force. These include people with physical disabilities, people with psychological difficulties, people with inadequate educational or training backgrounds, people with addiction problems and ex-offenders.

The project prefers clients with diverse histories and problems in order to avoid ghettoisation and negative dynamics and impact among clients. There are certain requirements of specific client groups.

For clients under 25 years of age, long-term unemployment is defined as unemployment for six months or more. For those over 25 years of age, long-term unemployment is defined as unemployment for one year or more.

4 Funding

The *AMS* and the European Social Fund provide 48% of project funding. Caritas raises 5% of the costs. The remaining costs are covered by the actual activities of the project (restaurant work).

Implementation

1 Services and delivery

Inigo offers 17 job placements in the restaurant. These include both kitchen and service staff. In addition, individuals who have been unable to complete a previous apprenticeship are welcomed into the project and assisted in completing their qualification. The average duration of employment is eight months and business hours are extended beyond the Austrian norm to allow for sufficient training time.

2 Accommodation

The project does not offer accommodation.

3 Integration

The project is primarily concerned with reintegration into the labour market although an individualised social assistance programme is also designed to meet clients' needs.

Outputs

1 Monitoring and evaluation

By contrast to the restaurant industry in general, which is experiencing decline, *Inigo* has demonstrated economic growth. This is particularly significant since *Inigo's* external funding from the *AMS* has not been adjusted in relation to inflation. Thus, even while its protected funding supply has declined in real terms, the project has been able to show economic growth.

An internal evaluation of success rates has been undertaken. If success is measured solely according to the individual's ability to find employment on the open labour market, then *Inigo* can show that 60% of its employees have successfully secured work. However, the AMS defines success more broadly to include the removal of barriers obstructing access to labour (for example, illiteracy). The success rate under this definition is 80%.

2 Problem areas

Four problem areas have been identified:
- The hybrid structure of the project combines social services provision with a commercial enterprise leading to both innovation in approach and complexity in administration. The project's status as an economic enterprise legally constrains its ability to hold assets or reserves. In turn, these legal constraints restrict the potential for investment which is necessary for longer-term productivity.
- High turnover, which is important within the context of the project's aims and objectives, is nonetheless a strain on productivity.
- The project lacks formal contractual arrangements.

• At present, success is measured primarily in financial terms with little evaluation of the social input element.

3 Dissemination

Unknown.

Case study 3

Country:	Belgium
Name of project:	*Les Agences Immobilières Sociales* (AIS) (Social Rental Agencies in Wallonia)
Location:	Throughout the Wallonia Region
Start date:	1993

Overview

This is not a single project but rather a regional initiative which is being developed by the voluntary sector with direct government funding and regulation through legislation. In recognition of the housing shortage, the growing demand for affordable housing and the constraints on meeting that demand through new construction, this initiative seeks to find housing solutions for homeless people in the private rental market. The *AIS* act as mediators between landlords and potential tenants while, at the same time, organising social support for those who need it. Although the *AIS* operate in the social sector, they are not social housing companies and do not draw profits from their work.

Innovation

This initiative is innovative for four reasons:

- Service provision operates within a legislative framework under which regional governments make a financial commitment to subsidise the work.
- The legislation calls for each agency to take an annual inventory of both the size of the homeless population within its area and the availability and condition of local housing stock. Special methods for determining both counts are being developed in conjunction with Brussels University under the coordinating auspices of the provincial government.
- The initiative seeks to address the acute housing crisis through the use of existing stock and, particularly, stock found in the private rented sector.
- The legislative framework for the AIS defines the nature of the tenancy between the landlord and the service user. The landlord–tenant

relationship is broadly based on the normal tenancy regimes. Nevertheless, the legislation recognises the particular circumstances of people with support needs and seeks to soften the more punitive aspects of mainstream tenancies.

Aims and objectives

The aim of the initiative is to encourage the use of existing stock in the private rental sector to house people who are homeless or at risk of being homeless. The objectives of the initiative are:

- to secure management contracts with private sector landlords and to establish tenancies between landlords and service users;
- to work in partnership with welfare agencies who can be called on to provide support to tenants as required;
- to work within the legislative framework and to draw on state subsidies to partially defray management costs.

Inputs

1 Agencies and partnerships

The *AIS* is not a single project but an initiative taken up by several different agencies. In 1996/97, 10 *AIS* were operating in the Wallonia Region and a further six or seven are expected to be launched in the near future. Each agency works with a number of private and public sector landlords as well as working with social welfare agencies to provide the required support for individuals. Two examples of *AIS* are *Gestion-Logement-Namur* and *Charleroi-Logement*.

The legislation requires each *AIS* to have a management committee on which sit representatives of a wide range of agencies. These include: the local authority and all local social services, CPAS, at least one local social housing company, representatives of the provincial government and of local authorities, representatives of local and community organisations, the tenants, the tenants association and the syndicate of landlords.

2 Areas and responsibility

Each *AIS* is responsible for identifying landlords in the private and public rental sectors and for negotiating management agreements with these landlords. Although the actual tenant holds the tenancy with the landlord, ensuring payment of rent is the responsibility of the *AIS* even where void conditions occur. Thus, the *AIS* acts as a facilitator enabling families and single people on low incomes to access housing at affordable rents while neutralising any of the risks for otherwise wary landlords. Where the condition of the accommodation is sub-standard, the *AIS* undertake renovation work usually involving the potential tenant as part of the training programme.

The *AIS* is responsible for organising any support services required by the client and, to this end, works with a number of social welfare agencies.

3 Target groups and numbers

The target groups for the *AIS* are households with low income. This is calculated as 50% higher than the maximum unemployment benefit. In 1996, the 10 operational *AIS* in Wallonia provided housing for a total of 416 households.

4 Funding

AIS are funded partially through their own activities and partially through government subsidies laid out in the 1996 legislation. The *AIS* requires tenants to pay a small premium on their rents to cover the costs of renovation and management. Sometimes, these costs are shared between the tenant and the landlord. In the first two years of their existence, *AIS* were to be subsidised by the regional government. Thereafter, the number of houses supplied determines the level of subsidy.

Implementation

1 Services and delivery

The *AIS* identify potential and appropriate landlords and act as mediators between these and prospective tenants. A range of social welfare agencies delivers the social support required.

2 Accommodation

The nature of the accommodation provided is determined by the individual's needs and by the availability of such accommodation. *AIS* vary widely in the number of houses they supply. Data from 1996 and 1997 suggests sizeable rates of growth (from a total of 309 houses to a total of 416 houses respectively). The accommodation is provided under two types of tenancies. Landlords with limited experience of working with this target group tend to offer short-term renewable tenancies. The second type of tenancy is offered for a nine-year period and follows the normal tenancy regime in Wallonia. However, recognising the spirit of *AIS* provision and the special problems which tenants may face, the legislative framework has established a modified tenancy model which removes some of the more punitive elements of the mainstream tenancy, particularly for breach of contract.

3 Integration

Unknown.

Outputs

1 Monitoring and evaluation

In 1993 the government introduced the *AIS* initiative. The amendments to the legislation in 1996 were the result of an evaluation of the overall system by the general board of accompaniment.

2 Problem areas

Unknown.

3 Dissemination

Unknown.

Case study 4

Country:	Belgium
Name of project:	*Iris*
Location:	Throughout the Brussels Capital Region
Start date:	1986

Overview

Iris was one of the first Social Rental Agencies (SRAs) in Brussels. It grew out of a reception house for homeless people. Recognising the difficulties of identifying appropriate accommodation both for itself and for its clients as well as the conflict of interest inherent in playing the dual role of landlord and support provider, the reception house sought to separate housing from support. This was achieved through the founding of a SRA on a voluntary basis.

Aims and objectives

The aims of the project are:
- to facilitate access to decent, affordable housing for people on low or no incomes in accordance with the constitutional right to decent housing enshrined in 1993;
- to separate housing from support in order to minimise the conflict of interest inherent in being landlord and support provider.

Innovation

This project is innovative because it is oriented towards meeting the diverse needs of vulnerable tenants. The separation of housing and support is achieved through cooperative working with social welfare agencies with housing acknowledged as the starting point, while insertion is seen as the target outcome.

Inputs

I Agencies and partnerships

Iris is a membership organisation made up of 19 agencies who offer a wide range of services to different target groups. *Iris* works with other complementary housing and welfare institutions.

2 Areas and responsibility

Iris manages housing stock which it rents from both the private and social housing sectors. The houses are sub-let to tenants at rents which are below the usual market prices.

    Iris was originally run wholly by volunteers. However, since the early 1990s one professional staff member was hired and, since 1996, a half-time administrator has been employed.

3 Target groups and numbers

Since *Iris* is a membership organisation, the target groups are those which are served by its members. The majority of people housed by *Iris* are on benefits or unemployment insurance with only 7% working under special statute or in training.

4 Funding

The Flemish community using funds from the Combat Against Poverty Programme covers staffing costs. Volunteers support paid workers. Some subsidies are used to cover the costs of rent deposits.

Implementation

I Services and delivery

Iris rents and purchases houses and makes them available to clients of its member organisations. Support is delivered by social welfare institutions to meet the individual's needs.

2 Accommodation

In total, *Iris* manages 82 housing units including four which it owns. In 1996, *Iris* managed 102 rent contracts housing 156 people.

3 Integration

Iris provides housing management support. Personal care and support services are provided by the member agencies who nominate individuals to *Iris*.

Outputs

1 Monitoring and evaluation

In 1996, 16 people left *Iris* to move to social housing (2), private rental (10), special aid (2) and another country (2). These figures suggest a small but important level of mobility.

2 Problem areas

It is difficult for tenants to eventually move into privately rented accommodation. Because of the high demand for the services of the SRA and the limited ability of sitting tenants to flow through, entrance for new tenants is becoming more limited. Nevertheless, a tenancy in an *Iris* property can help tenants to bridge the waiting time for social rental housing. For others, the financial possibility of moving into private rental accommodation may develop.

3 Dissemination

Unknown.

Case study 5

Country:	Belgium
Project name:	*Sociale verhuurkantoren (SVK)* (The Social Rental Agencies in Flanders)
Location:	Throughout Flanders
Start date:	1993

Overview

By the mid–to–late 1980s, welfare workers in Flanders were recognising the growing housing problems of their clients and seeing these in combination with material, legal and psycho-social problems. In order to tackle the multi-dimensional problems with which they were being presented, a coordinated approach was required. This would maximise the use of existing services while creating new services to meet identified gaps.

SVKs are not a single project but rather a regional initiative which is carried out by several different agencies throughout Flanders. They grew out of the organisation of the welfare sector and housing activism. Although the roots of the *SVKs* are firmly planted outside the statutory sector, there have been some important contributions by local authorities. For example, in 1994 the province of Oost-Vlaanderen launched an initiative to provide organisational and financial support to *SVKs* working to meet the housing needs of poor people. This was a departure from its usual marginal involvement in housing policy.

Aims and objectives

The aims of the *SVKs* are:
• to improve the housing situation for particular social groups through access to housing in the private rental sector;
• to detect and highlight any dysfunction in the housing market with particular emphasis on the limits or disadvantages for tenants in the private rental sector.

Innovation

SVKs are considered innovative because they seek housing solutions for people on low incomes in the private sector. Through a system of rent guarantees, they mobilise private sector landlords to provide housing for people whom they might otherwise not serve and, in this way, work to address the acute housing crisis in Flanders.

Inputs

1 Agencies and partnerships

A range of different *SVKs* operates in Flanders. Each *SVK* is a cooperative body of different institutions, services and organisations who are working with the same kind of client group in a broad, but nevertheless definable geographic area. *SVKs* work in partnership with both the landlords in the private sector and the nominating agencies who provide the support. In addition, the legal conventions governing the *SVKs* require them to operate within existing networks in their local area.

2 Areas and responsibility

SVKs are responsible for prospecting for potential houses, negotiating leases with the landlord and/or purchasing houses. The *SVK* has responsibility for all aspects of housing management. Unlike other landlords, it seeks to remedy tenancy issues such as non-payment of rents or anti-social behaviour through individualised support work provided by the nominating service. If, despite support, tenancy problems persist, reinstitutionalisation is considered.

    SVK also organises rent deposits (often through the local social services who provide limited rent subsidies) and furniture.

3 Target groups and numbers

The target groups are marginalised persons who need aftercare support services when leaving an institution or treatment centre. These include single persons, people on benefits, ethnic minorities, single parents and homeless people. The founding members of the organisation according to their own client groups determine the specific target group for each *SVK*. Two thirds of households housed by the SVKs are single persons with or without children. The remainder of the households are families, couples living together or married. Three quarters of *SVK* tenants are unemployed.

4 Funding

SVKs which are recognised by the government and are working within the convention framework are eligible for subsidies for their operational costs including staff costs. Where the properties rented are listed, a wide range of subsidies is available for renovation work.

Some *SVKs* are recognised but not wholly subsidised by the Flemish government. For these *SVKs*, subsidies to cover operational costs may be accessed through urban policy legislation. If they let more than 50 houses, *SVKs* may also be eligible for subsidies under the convention governing their work.

The usual annual subsidy for *SVKs* is €45,860 for staff and a further €12,395 for running costs. This amount can rise by a further €9,915 if the number of houses managed exceeds 50 and cooperation between agencies is demonstrated.

Implementation

I Services and delivery

The primary activity of the *SVKs* is the letting or sub-letting of houses to people who have formerly lived in institutions or to persons who are at risk of being reinstitutionalised.

Clients are nominated to the *SVKs* by different institutions. Nominating institutions undertake the provision of support services to the client in their new home. The selection criteria is based on a priority system which considers the source of income, the number of children, the rehousing needs and the employment situation of the candidate. Applications are awarded points and the chronology of application is considered.

2 Accommodation

The *SVK* either rents or purchases properties. For properties rented in the private sector, *SVKs* enter into lease agreements with the landlords. Properties are subsequently sub-let to *SVK* clients. The *SVKs* operate within the federal law on private renting but the conditions for sub-letting are laid down by the Flemish government. Thus, *SVKs* are obligated to work within the boundaries set up by the social rental system.

3 Integration

Housing provided by the *SVKs* is intended to be long-term or at least for the term of the tenancy arrangement according to the sub-let. Under federal housing legislation two types of contracts between the landlord and the *SVK* are possible: the long lease (nine years), and the short lease. In addition, infinite and other very lengthy leases are possible. The majority of leases negotiated between landlords and *SVKs* are long or infinite leases (70%). In turn, just over half of all sub-lets are offered on a long let basis (52% for nine years, 3% infinite). The use of the short let for tenants is seen as a tool in helping tenants to move on.

Social insertion to meet the individual's needs is developed and delivered by the nominating institution or agency.

Outputs

1 Monitoring and evaluation

The results of the self-evaluation of the nine conventions *SVKs* show:
* a rise in the number of houses rented;
* improvement in the quality of houses rented;
* movement of tenants onto permanent housing;
* good development of support networks;
* willingness on the part of landlords to offer houses;
* the guarantee system offered by the *SVKs* places them in a good negotiating position with landlords;
* security and stability for tenants as a result of the use of long leases;
* an evolution from care for the dwelling to care for the people;
* a rising legitimacy accorded to the *SVKs*.

The self-evaluation also highlights certain problem areas:
* professionalism has not been wholly achieved;
* the *SVK* model remains a temporary solution;
* although rising, the number of houses available still fails to meet demand;
* problems with the quality and renovation of properties;

- high rents;
- rent arrears;
- the support is minimal since the housing dimension dominates;
- social housing companies may have ambiguous attitudes towards *SVKs*;
- lack of financial room for the development of the *SVKs*.

2 Problem areas

Finding suitable housing in good condition to rent on the private rental market is a problem. The search for appropriate housing units is time-consuming and causes delays. Once obtained, housing may be sub-standard and may require considerable renovation. Although this does provide a good training opportunity, it also causes further delays and has cost implications. Once housed, tenants' length of stay may be determined by the landlord who may break the agreement.

SVKs have to operate within the market-led private rental sector which impacts on the levels of rent. The length of contracts is determined by a combination of federal and regional legislation. The requirement to comply by both these legislative frameworks impacts on both affordability and security of tenure.

3 Dissemination

Unknown.

Case study 6

Country:	Denmark
Name of project:	*Gå Ud Projektet – Mændenes Hjem*
Location:	Copenhagen – Vesterbro
Start date:	1995

Overview

Gå Ud is a resettlement programme associated with the *Mændenes Hjem* (a temporary shelter for homeless men). Copenhagen Municipality, under Paragraph 105 of the Social Security Act, provides the *Mændeness Hjem*. It is a holding place before residents are moved on to a place of permanent residence such as an appropriate institution or a place of their own. *Gå Ud Projektet* works with shelter residents, housing departments and housing associations to secure permanent housing and provide support.

Aims and objectives

The *Mændenes Hjem* project aims to resettle residents on a permanent basis in a secure and stable residence. This can be an institution or a flat.

The primary aim of the *Gå Ud Projekt* is successful resettlement in a flat. Minor aims of the *Gå Ud Projekt* include:

- skill transfer and confidence building in dealing with authority and bureaucracy;
- the encouragement of self-confidence, self-esteem and motivation in clients.

Innovation

The project is considered innovative because it provides a personalised reintegration programme with comprehensive guidance and support, including the provision of aftercare services.

Inputs

1 Agencies and partnerships

The local municipality is the umbrella organisation and provides the main funding components of the *Mændenes Hjem*. Central government provides funding for the *Gå Ud* project worker. The social work department, the housing department and housing associations provide the flats.

2 Areas and responsibility

The Hjem employs 20 full-time staff who work with residents during their stay in the shelter. The *Gå Ud Projekt* employs a full-time support worker who is attached to the *Hjem*. The *Gå Ud* worker has specific responsibility for encouraging, aiding and facilitating resettlement of residents from the temporary shelter to a home of their own.

The *Gå Ud* worker arranges resettlement in conjunction with *Hjem* residents. The project worker is responsible for overseeing all phases of this process. These include: registration and application to the municipal housing department or other housing agency, assistance in negotiating offers of flats, organisation of finance and furniture for the flat and follow-up work once the resident is settled.

3 Target groups and numbers

Originally the *Mændenes Hjem* provided shelter for 83 homeless men with alcohol and drug abuse problems. Today, it caters for large numbers of refugees and immigrants, many of whom have problems of alcoholism and drug abuse. A 1996 profile indicated that 20% of residents had alcohol problems, 60% had drug problems, 15% had mental health problems and 5% had other problems. A total of 60% of service users are Danish citizens while the remaining 40% are either immigrants or refugees. Admission criteria require individuals to have an address in Copenhagen or to have been accepted as Copenhagen Municipality's responsibility.

4 Funding

The Ministry of Social Affairs pays for the *Gå Ud* worker. *Mændenes Hjem* itself is funded one seventh by users (from their social welfare/

benefits payments) and six sevenths by the municipality. The state reimburses the municipality for 75% of the costs of the shelter.

Implementation

1 Services and delivery

Mændenes Hjem provides temporary stay accommodation for 83 men suffering from alcohol and drug problems. The maximum length of stay is six months. The emphasis is on resettlement in a permanent stay institution which will provide appropriate support in their own flat.

The *Gå Ud Projekt* employs one full-time staff member whose role is to act as an advocate for residents who wish to move into their own flat. At reception, a profile of the new resident is compiled based on background history, sources of income and the nature of the resident's problems. An introduction to the *Mændenes Hjem* and the surrounding area is provided. The *Gå Ud* worker takes responsibility for registering the resident with the municipal housing department and with appropriate housing associations. The *Gå Ud* worker's duties include:

- working systematically with the person with the intention of easing him out of the home;
- working in cooperation with the individual to establish contact with relevant institutions capable of providing a dwelling and persisting with applications through regular follow-up visits;
- ensuring attendance at meetings and interviews, assisting residents in organising a regular life-style and ensuring adherence to a semblance of time discipline;
- acting as a liaison between the resident and external bodies such as social workers, doctors, and mental health centres and drugs treatment centres;
- generally acting as an advocate for the resident;
- once an apartment has been found, assisting with the negotiation of finances from social security and the acquisition of furniture;
- assisting in establishing contacts in the new place of residence and familiarising the resident with his new environment;
- providing aftercare services which involve follow-up visits while being careful to avoid interference;
- maintaining momentum and motivation throughout the process.

2 Accommodation

The *Mændenes Hjem* offers 83 places. Nine of these are single rooms (reserved for the worst cases); the remainder are double rooms. There is 24-hour access to the shelter.

3 Integration

See above – 'Areas and responsibility' and 'Services and delivery'.

Outputs

1 Monitoring and evaluation

No resettlement targets are identified.

2 Problem areas

Four problem areas can be identified:

- *Gå Ud Projektet's* funding for 1998 is not fully guaranteed, with only six months of funding secured. Therefore the project's future is in question unless Copenhagen Municipality continues to fund it.
- There has been rapid turnover in *Gå Ud* employees – three in as many years. This situation leads to lack of familiarity with the set-up and procedures and with effective aftercare.
- The project's focus is on resettlement into flats, thereby ignoring other alternatives such as shared dwellings. The implicit question being raised is whether resettlement in a tenanted flat is always desirable.
- Relocation in an area which may be unfamiliar can create problems and feelings of isolation and alienation. On the other hand, such relocation can also have the advantage of breaking the substance abuse network.

3 Dissemination

Unknown.

Case study 7

Country:	Finland
Name of project:	*Jyvaskyla Street Mission*
Location:	City of Jyvaskyla
Start date:	1954

Overview

This project provides shelter, short–term and permanent housing to people with substance abuse problems.

Aims and objectives:

The aim of the project is to provide housing for people with substance abuse problems. The housing services provided are designed to meet the realities of clients' lives.

Innovation

The project is considered innovative because it recognises that homelessness and substance abuse are two distinct problems. It forms a departure from the usual housing projects which stipulate preconditions such as sobriety or good behaviour as prerequisites to accessing housing. Instead, the *Street Mission* offers housing to homeless persons despite their serious abuse problems. Once housed, tenants who create severe disturbances are temporarily moved to an adjacent shelter. However, the project differs from other similar initiatives in that persons temporarily excluded are allowed to regain access to their keys instead of embarking on a cycle of emergency housing in shelters or hostels.

Inputs

1 Agencies and partnerships

The *Street Mission* is the direct service provider. The municipalities act as partners by financing and purchasing the services in an enabler/ purchaser role.

2 Areas and responsibility

The project sells its housing services under purchasing agreements to the city and rural districts.

3 Target groups and numbers

The project's target group is people with substance abuse problems. It provides 120 dwellings for single men and women with drug/alcohol problems as well as families. The *Mission* accommodates approximately 200 people each year.

4 Funding

Funding comes from various sources. In 1997, the city purchased housing services valued at €336,200 and rural district €51,700. Finance also comes from the Slot Machine Association, business development centres, the Jyvaskyla Development Company and EU projects.

Residents pay rent which varies according to the size of the accommodation. Some residents are eligible for housing allowance while others contribute through payments made directly from unemployment and living allowances.

Implementation

1 Services and delivery

The *Mission* provides a day centre, emergency shelter and permanent housing.

2 Accommodation

The *Mission* provides different types of accommodation to meet individual needs:

- *Ensiaskel* day centre offers emergency night shelter of 16 beds as well as 51 apartments with Tenancy Act rental agreements; these apartments are state-subsidised social housing;
- *Takakaiton* day centre offers 27 independent apartments for persons released from institutions for substance abuse and those released from prison with substance abuse problems;

- three halfway houses offer a total of 30 beds where tenants sign rental agreements; the apartments are clusters of four rooms with a communal kitchen and are intended for clients aiming at abstention;
- *Nurmela* Home is a temperance unit of 11 beds for single people and families; apartments are again clusters of single rooms with a communal kitchen; this provision is run on a Christian philosophy and is 'suitable only for persons wishing to change their lives through faith';
- *Neverending Story* is the Walkers café in the city centre aimed at under 25s; it has one emergency apartment.

3 Integration

Unknown.

Outputs

1 Monitoring and evaluation

Yet to be undertaken.

2 Problem areas

The *Mission* has identified a growing number of people with drug-related problems who are in need of housing. However, working with drug addicts will require new methods. This area is being considered by the *Street Mission* but has yet to be fully developed.

3 Dissemination

The model is local.

Case study 8

Country:	Finland
Name of project:	*Supported Housing Project of the Y-Foundation*
Location:	Nationwide
Start date:	1985 for Y-Foundation

Overview

The *Y-Foundation* was established to provide housing for homeless people and refugees in Finland. The Association of Finnish Local Authorities, five of the main cities, the Finnish Red Cross, the Finnish Association for Mental Health, the state alcohol monopoly (ALKO) and the central construction employers and workers unions, founded it.

This project forms part of the *Y-Foundation's* overall work providing permanent housing with individualised support packages for homeless people who may or may not have special needs. The housing is purchased or rented by the *Y-Foundation* from the existing stock of housing companies and made available to clients of local authorities and church organisations. The support is provided by a number of NGOs and special needs agencies. The project operates under tri-partite contractual agreements.

Aims and objectives

The aim of the project is to provide permanent housing and support for homeless people to enable them to live independently.

Innovation

The project is considered innovative because support in everyday life is provided in normal flats to people who would otherwise have difficulty in living independently in ordinary housing. The project therefore allows for normalisation leading to independent living.

Inputs

1 Agencies and partnerships

The *Y-Foundation*, local authorities and voluntary organisations are all involved in the project. The *Y-Foundation* works on the principle of providing goal–oriented services founded on agreements. The municipality, the NGO and the *Y-Foundation* sign these tri–partite agreements. Partnerships are based on a contractual model between local authorities, *Y-Foundation* and other NGOs (see below under 'Services and delivery').

2 Areas and responsibility

The *Y-Foundation* concentrates on the purchase and maintenance of real estate. Most of the accommodation is placed at the disposal of the local authorities and church organisations which select the occupants and provide the support and any other services required.

The level of need for supported housing in the municipality is estimated jointly by social welfare, healthcare authorities and *Y-Foundation*.

The Finnish Association for Mental Health is responsible for the coordination, training and running of the support person system. A board of representatives from all the organisations involved supervises their operations.

3 Target groups and numbers

The broad target group for the *Y-Foundation's* work is single homeless people who have difficulty obtaining a home by themselves on the free market. Within this broad target context, specific attention is paid to clients with mental health problems who are in need of housing and support and who are referred by the mental health office or care unit. Special attention is also paid to young people and others newly embarking on an independent life in a home of their own.

In total, the *Y-Foundation* provides 3,700 apartments in 46 municipalities across Finland. In 1997 there were about 100 supported clients and 150 supporters. The supported housing scheme is a new initiative and, as such, currently serves only a small proportion of people living in *Y-Foundation* flats. The process of identifying other *Y-Foundation* clients in need of support is ongoing.

4 Funding

Financial assistance is provided for the purchase of housing by the state, by the Slot Machine Association and the local authorities with which the *Y-Foundation* cooperates. Low-interest state and bank loans are available to the project.

Implementation

1 Services and delivery

Y-Foundation purchases good standard small apartments from the existing stock of ordinary housing companies. Local authorities and voluntary organisations provide the support services required. Since 1994, the Finnish Association for Mental Health, the Association for Relatives and Friends of Mental Health Rehabilitees and the Helmi Mental Health Association have been providing housing support services.

Each person is assigned a personal helper. Support service agreements are individually designed with joint consultation between the client, the support worker and the person in charge of voluntary support services in the locality.

2 Accommodation

Accommodation consists of small apartments in existing housing schemes and dispersed in the stock. Tenants have a tenancy under the Tenancy Act which is not linked to the duration of the support.

At the beginning of 1998 13 localities in Finland offered supported housing run by the Finnish Association for Mental Health. The *Y-Foundation* provided housing in six of these localities.

3 Integration

Full tenancies are provided in permanent housing not linked to the support programme. Living with others in a condominium provides opportunities for social integration.

Outputs

1 Monitoring and evaluation

Informal feedback from clients has highlighted the importance of the support service to those receiving it. Although no proper follow-up studies have yet been undertaken, there are signs that people receiving support cope better than average in their housing.

Reassessment of the appropriateness of support levels to meet individual needs are an integral part of the 'support service agreement' and the intervals for reassessment are indicated therein.

2 Problem areas

The reliance on voluntary work in the provision of support services creates problems since the demand for such services is not sufficiently met by the supply of voluntary workers.

3 Dissemination

In 1997, the *Y-Foundation* initiated a supported housing project in four towns – Helsinki, Espoo, Turku and Tampere – to expand its services.

Case study 9

Country:	France
Name of project:	*La Roche sur Yon Project*
Location:	La Roche sur Yon (Vendée)
Start date:	1995

Overview

This project maximises the use and effectiveness of existing services for homeless people by developing a strong partnership between a wide range of statutory and voluntary agencies. The agencies provide a range of housing and support services and the emphasis is on allowing service users choice in selecting the services which are most appropriate to their needs.

Aims and objectives

The project aims to:
• develop solidarity with homeless people who are alone and in difficulty;
• develop a common understanding of the local processes of social exclusion;
• promote good community relations in order to relieve some of the local tension and intolerance;
• maintain diversity in service provision in order to provide service users with choice.

The objectives of the project are:
• to organise and coordinate existing services in the area in order to provide service users with a diverse yet integrated series of options to meet their various and complex needs;
• to commission action research to identify the needs of service users and map out existing services, and establish a methodology for their effective coordination.

Innovation

The project is considered innovative because it organises existing services, develops effective partnerships between statutory and voluntary sector organisations and responds to the global needs of the individual while respecting diversity in the individual's potential for choice. Effective partnership working between statutory and voluntary sector agencies is a departure from the norm in France.

Inputs

1 Agencies and partnerships

A wide range of agencies, both statutory and voluntary, are involved in the organisation and delivery of the services. These include the DDASS, the police, the *CCAS (Centre Communal d'Action Sociale)*, the *FAJ*, national associations *(le Secours Catholique, la Sauvegarde de l'Enfance, Saint-Vincent* teams and *Aides)*, local associations already managing reception centres and housing *(l'Etoile, la Halte)* and specific programmes undertaken by different agencies such as *Graine d'ID, SEL* and *la Marmite*.

In addition, resource centres, befriending services, health action projects and other multi-purpose activities in the project area are involved on a needs-led basis.

The agencies involved have explicitly avoided a single access point system in order to respect the complexity of individual needs. Instead, the project is guided by a multi-faceted approach based on flexibility and a common level of understanding shared by all partners.

The project operates a loosely constructed partnership model with the *DDASS* taking the lead in the creation of the project and the coordination of the day reception centre. The effectiveness of partnership working has been attributed to the collaborative approach adopted by each member without a need to defend each agency's territory. Partnership working has enabled each agency to develop a broader understanding and awareness of the multi-faceted issues of social exclusion while at the same time safeguarding each agency's autonomy.

The mobilisation of statutory agencies such as the *DDASS*, the *CAF* and the *CCAS* signals a departure from the norm in France where statutory agencies are seldom inclined to work in true partnership with voluntary sector agencies and with the associations. The broader interpretation of legislative frameworks for the delivery of services has enabled statutory agencies to become proper partners.

Service users are also partners in the project. This approach is consistent with the global view of the individual which forms an integral part of the project ethos.

2 Areas and responsibility

Each agency is responsible for the delivery of its established services. The *DDASS* is responsible for the employment of the project coordinator whose role is to facilitate interagency working and dialogue.

3 Target groups and numbers

Given the multi-faceted approach of the project and its foundation on existing rather than new service provision, the target groups are very broad. They include roofless people, people with mental health problems, and homeless people requiring a certain degree of support to live independently in the community.

There is no data on the number of individuals served by the project and it is likely that such data would be difficult to collect given the multi-faceted approach and the diversity of services over a wide geographic area.

4 Funding

The project is funded by the *DDASS* although the active coordination of services is due to finish in 1998 since it is perceived that the ensemble is working well and the role of a coordinator is now superfluous.

Implementation

1 Services and delivery

The project at *La Roche sur Yon* offers diverse services to marginalised people. These include:

- reception – orientation evaluates winter shelters as well as the activities of *Solidar'été*; this service also provides a number of reception centres in various locations leaving the choice to the individual;
- groupe *Santé-Hygiène* is primarily concerned with mental health issues and develops partnerships with psychiatric services for service users;

- *la Marmite* unites the different local food services and seeks to diversify the provision of alimentation services beyond the traditional food bank model; *la Marmite* has established systems for bulk ordering and delivery of products under the management of service users themselves; it has also established communal kitchens and works with associations and the *CAF*;
- work-training opportunities are available through such agencies as *Secours Catholique* which runs a community grocery;
- data on existing services is centrally gathered and made available to all members;
- training is provided for all volunteers;
- *Solidar'été* provides emergency housing in the summer months when winter shelters are closed; it also provides assistance with food provision as well as summer work for residents;
- '*mini-guides*' are prepared by a number of partners and provide information on all issues relevant to service users including emergency shelters, support, health, food and leisure;
- *Pension de Famille* provides warm shelters to house individuals on a long-term basis who are capable of some degree of autonomy but may not yet be ready for HLM-type housing;
- the annual week-long conference gives service users a voice and raises awareness of the issues among the population at large.

2 Accommodation

The majority of the accommodation provided within the context of the project is short-term and seen as emergency shelter. This includes winter shelters as well as summer shelters. One of the partners provides long-term accommodation for people with low-level support needs. None of the agencies specifically responds to long-term housing and resettlement needs.

3 Integration

Some of the partners involved in the project provide services aimed at reintegration. These include some level of job training, work during the summer months, access to healthcare needs and service user involvement in both management and decision-making processes. The underlying philosophy of the project is based on the empowerment of the individual through the respect of diversity and, as such, aims at breaking down the barriers which isolate marginalised people through direct channelling.

Outputs

I Monitoring and evaluation

To be carried out.

2 Problem areas

Problem areas have been kept to a minimum by the active participation and cooperative spirit of each partner agency.

3 Dissemination

This networking model is in the process of developing. There is no actual framework; rather the work is based on the will and interest of partner agencies.

Case study 10

Country:	France
Name of project:	*Association Nivernaise d'Accueil et de Réinsertion (ANAR)*
Location:	Nevers
Start date:	1974

Overview

This project focuses on reinsertion in the labour market for people who have been in trouble with the law and for those who have experienced exclusion from the labour market. The project provides training and work experience in skills appropriate to the local environment. It also works with other agencies who provide transitional housing and supports service users to find long-term housing solutions.

Aims and objectives

The aim of the project is to prevent patterns of re-offending through a balanced integration programme for ex-offenders and accused persons. The objectives of the project are:

- to provide meaningful and appropriate work for both men and women who have been in trouble with the law in order to give them a sense of responsibility, a role in their society and confidence in their abilities as citizens;
- to facilitate access to housing for the individuals above.

Innovation

The innovation is in the approach to this particular target group (ex-offenders, those in semi-confinement and those who are awaiting trial). The project combines a strict sense of discipline as required by the judiciary with an organised skilled labour training which is appropriate for the local environment and economy.

Inputs

1 Agencies and partnerships

The *ANAR* is the principal organisation delivering and coordinating the work of the project. Other agencies include penal institutions, social action agencies of the state and the départements, elected representatives, the associations, the HLM and the communes.

2 Areas and responsibility

The *ANAR* is responsible for organising work initiatives including negotiating with environmental management agencies for placements of service users and the overall management of the sewing workshop. In addition, *ANAR* works in partnership with the HLMs to organise access to housing.

3 Target groups and numbers

The initial target group was restricted to accused persons but was later expanded to include ex-offenders and those in semi-confinement. The project is also open to women who are excluded from the labour force whether or not they have been involved with the criminal justice system.

4 Funding

Financed by *DDASS*, the prison service and the département.

Implementation

1 Services and delivery

The principal services focus on job training and employment as a means of reintegration into the socioeconomic fabric. Activities include environmental work (bush clearing work, forestry, etc) and a sewing workshop. The former is for men while the latter is for women. Both work placements include a formal training element and, in the case of the sewing workshop, the work is remunerated.

2 *Accommodation*

Housing is organised in partnership with local HLMs. Although service users cannot stay in the same accommodation permanently, long-term accommodation is generally found within the same neighbourhood in order to retain the continuity of community links.

In some cases, service users may actually live in the prison with daily exits to participate in the project. On the other hand, service users who are still under probation may live in semi–secure accommodation where their movement is restricted outside of work hours. The purpose of the accommodation in this case is to provide an alternative to imprisonment and to enable the service user to take some initial steps towards integration in anticipation of their release.

3 *Integration*

Integration is primarily seen in terms of labour market insertion. The skills learned are professionally taught and are appropriate to the local setting. For example, the environmental work is particularly appropriate in Nevers, a rural area with long-term employment possibilities in forestry work.

Outputs

1 *Monitoring and evaluation*

To be undertaken.

2 *Problem areas*

Unknown.

3 *Dissemination*

France has a number of projects which cater for people leaving penal institutions. This project differs from the other similar programmes in the quality of the insertion work it offers.

Case study 11

Country:	France
Name of project:	*Relais Soleil Tourquenois (RST)*
Location:	Tourcoing (Lille in the North of France)
Start date:	Not known

Overview

This project was created to address the needs of the individual/family in the least disruptive way by removing the obstacles which require successive moves and replacing them with the possibility of continuity in the same location but with varying levels of support to meet their individual needs.

Aims and objectives

The aim of the project is to minimise the disruptions to family life created by the necessity of regular moves from one accommodation to another.

Innovation

The project is considered innovative because it introduces a sliding status for the resident and the accommodation as opposed to the more traditional physical change in location and type of accommodation. The latter is the common path for access to permanent housing which is funnelled through a complex system of moves from emergency to medium-term and on to long-term/permanent accommodation. This project provides stability for service users through a seamless service.

Inputs

1 Agencies and partnerships

The association *Relais Soleil Tourquenois* is the principal service provider. *RST* works with local agencies providing specialised services. These include *Emmaus* and *Secours Catholique* who assist in accessing furniture.

HLMs and private landlords also work in partnership with the project by providing the accommodation.

2 Areas and responsibility

HLMs and private landlords make the accommodation available to RST clients. *RST* provides support services.

3 Target groups and numbers

Unknown.

4 Funding

Financed by the state and the département, plus furniture funding under system D.

Implementation

1 Services and delivery

The association rents the accommodation either from HLMs or from a private landlord. The rent is paid through the *ALT* (*allocation logement temporaire*) for the initial six months. Thereafter, rent is paid through the *AL* (*allocation logement*) or *APL* (*allocation personnelle logement*) and the resident becomes a sub-tenant. Finally, the tenancy can be transferred directly to the tenant in their own right and the association asks the HLM or private landlord for another property. This model allows for a more effective packaging of integration initiatives and shortens the time required to accede to permanent housing. It suppresses the successive ruptures in provision which are evident in the typical model and thus provides a seamless service.

2 Accommodation

The project aims to provide accommodation in reasonable condition. This is particularly important since service users need to develop a commitment and an attachment to the accommodation which is intended as permanent housing. The success of the tenancy depends in large measure on securing suitable housing in good condition.

The accommodation is intended as permanent housing for service users with a change in their status and that of the accommodation rather than an actual move from one place to another.

3 Integration

The needs of the service user are met by the *RST*. The level of support provided should decrease as the service user moves from occupant status to becoming a full tenant in their own right. The pace of change in status is dictated by the ability and resources of the service user rather than as a set programme.

Outputs

1 Monitoring and evaluation

The project is very new.

2 Problem areas

The principal problem areas in the project are the access to funding for the provision of support services, the renovation of properties, and the purchase of furniture and administrative work. Other difficulties encountered include:
- the identification of suitable accommodation in good condition;
- relations with local inhabitants who may feel threatened by the placement of families with socioeconomic difficulties in their neighbourhood;
- cumbersome administrative structures.

3 Dissemination

The project is very new.

Case study 12

Country:	Germany
Name of project:	*Soziale Wohnraumhilfe* (*SWH*) (Organisation for Housing and Social Assistance)
Location:	Hanover, Lower Saxony
Start date:	Initiated in 1989, opened in May 1991

Overview

This project provides permanent housing for single homeless people who are leaving institutions.

Aims and objectives

The aim of the project is to rehouse single homeless people in permanent housing with normal tenancies and to prove that such provision is more cost-effective than more short-term accommodation.

The project has several objectives. These are:

- to provide an incentive to private investors such as building societies to provide housing for single homeless people; the incentives offered are financial as well as church land;
- to create a new special department of the Central Advice Office (*SWH*) which would administer housing;
- to rent dwellings through the *SWH* and to subsequently sub-let these to single homeless people on the basis of a rent guarantee system to the owner-builder;
- to organise individual care packages to be supplied by separate agencies.

Innovation

The project is considered innovative because it calls for the *SWH* to act as an intermediary agency between the building company, the social care agencies and the church to assemble and manage housing projects for single homeless people using both new build, conversion and existing housing. The project allows single homeless people in need of social support to rent normal self-contained dwellings with full tenancy rights with permanent tenure.

Inputs

1 Agencies and partnerships

The principal agency is *Soziale Wohnraumhilfe* which is one department of the Central Advice Office for Single Homeless Persons in Hanover. *COA* is an organisational branch of *Diakonisches Werk Hanover*. *Diakonisches Werk Hanover* is a service provider offering homes and services for homeless people. It is also a welfare agency drawing membership from other legally independent institutions for homeless people and for other target groups.

SWH cooperates with the different social work services and institutions for the homeless in Hanover and enters into agreements for the provision of services and social support. Building societies are partners of SWH in construction projects, procuring a proportion of the financing and acting as builder owners. Upon completion of construction, the building societies let the dwellings out to SWH who subsequently rent it out to homeless people. SWH offers cheap credit or low price leases of land and so on as incentives for building societies. Moreover, they take responsibility for administration and tenancy risks.

SWH also accesses housing stock through partnership with parishes and other housing owners who lease stock to the project for sub-letting to homeless people. SWH cooperates closely with the municipal authorities.

2 Areas and responsibility

As defined above. SWH acts as intermediary between finance institutions, housing company and social services agencies.

3 Target groups and numbers

The target group is single homeless people with extraordinary difficulties. Initially only those who had formerly been in homeless institutions were accepted into the project. However, more recently, people who had received ambulant services have also been accepted.

Funding from the Land as well as the City of Hanover allows the project to cater for the single homeless of Hanover as well as 'persons without a settled way of living' (for example, people coming from outside Hanover) who fall under the responsibility of the Land. The project currently caters for 114 people. *SWH* is planning to open new projects.

4 Funding

Funding is primarily through normal private investment and public subsidies but also includes church donations and funds as well as gifts of land.

At the end of 1996, the total cost of the 114 flats built or planned was €7.44 million which was met from state subsidies (52%), builder-owners and banks (40%) and church funds and donations (8%).

The Land, the City of Hanover and the church each contribute around one third of the annual operating costs (personnel and non-personnel – revenue funding) which amounts to €158,000. Financial losses due to rent arrears and refurbishment after disappearance or death of tenants can be met by a risk guarantee from the Protestant church (€4,600 in 1997).

A total of 58% of building costs were loans from the Land, 26% from housing company capital and 16% from capital market loan. Rents were high because public subsidies still allow a relatively high rent level and because there are a number of additional costs to the basic rent.

Implementation

1 Services and delivery

Housing with normal tenancies is allocated by *SWH* under an agreement with the municipal housing office of Hanover (based on a 25-year agreement).

2 Accommodation

Currently, 56 dwellings are provided and a further 58 dwellings are either at the planning or construction stage giving a total of 114 dwellings. All accommodation is self-contained single-person flats.

3 Integration

Support is provided based on personal capacities. The accommodation is offered under normal tenancies.

Outputs

1 Monitoring and evaluation

One part of the project was evaluated between 1994 and 1996. The evaluation of the H13 scheme was conducted using interviews and other qualitative methods. The following were interviewed: *SWH* staff, managers of the housing company, homeless tenants, care and social work staff, neighbours, municipality and Land staff.

Of the total of 12 flats in the H13 scheme evaluated, 16 people were housed in the first 2.5 years of evaluation. In the overall project, only nine out of 57 rehousing tenancies have failed and only one of these involved eviction. It is likely that people who have failed as *SWH* tenants will have a poor chance of being accepted by other landlords. *SWH* determines its own acceptance criteria and the project is under no obligation to rehouse those who have been evicted. By the same token, the project may choose to give an evicted tenant a second chance.

Compared to costs involved in maintaining someone in an institution, the costs involved are approximately half of the costs of homeless institutions (estimated as €1,809 per month). Costs are evaluated as follows:

	€/month
Enhanced housing management	96.5
Acquisition costs to *SWH*	30.5
Social care	244.2
Rent, heat and light	292.0
Social welfare living costs	276.8
Total	940.0

2 Problem areas

The main problem areas highlighted were:

- The amount, nature and funding of social care and the cooperation between housing management and social care. There have been disagreements between *SWH* and social workers about the extent, form and nature of social care required. This can be seen as the 'traditional conflict situation between landlord and social worker'. On the one hand, *SWH* expects active and permanent care; on the other hand, social workers see their role more as counsel acting on the clients' instructions. With 60 tenancies directly arranged by *SWH* so far, about half required regular need for care which involved *SWH* staff.

- The time-limited nature of funding of social care coupled with the institutions' unwillingness/inability to accept responsibility for care provision beyond the agreed funding period creates difficulties in maintaining care and support services. At end of the two-and-a-half year evaluation, only four of the 12 original tenants continued to receive care from outside. The level of care decreased after one year (one to three hours per month). The initial prognosis/assessment made by social workers was often wrong. Thus, with respect to the provision of social care which accompanies housing and is seen as an essential part of integration, it was considered that the "organisation, financing and quality of social care for rehoused homeless persons has to be improved considerably".

Those who had lived in institutions for a long time found the self-contained flats isolating but there were indications that this changed over time. The majority of tenants remain unemployed so, "for most of them rehousing put an end to homelessness but not to exclusion from the labour market".

The separation of housing management and social care which was originally planned could not be sustained because "SWH has to bear the economic risk of tenancies".

Problem issues with tenants changed over time. Initially, the issues related to financial debt and furnishing of flats. Later on they revolved around training, jobs and social relations/addiction.

3 Dissemination

The project has been the subject of detailed evaluation, the results of which have been published. In addition, *Soziale Wohnraumhilfe* functions as an advice agency for similar projects outside Hanover. It has helped to fund similar agencies in other locales.

Case study 13

Country:	Germany
Name of project:	*Wohnung statt Heimplatz* (Stable Housing in Place of Shelters)
Location:	Bielefeld, North Rhine-Wesphalia
Start date:	Initial preparations – 1992
	Conversion etc – 1994 and 1997

Overview

This project provides permanent housing and support for people who have a long-term history of homelessness. There is a separation of housing and support where housing is made available through the conversion of existing accommodation and the construction of new units and support is provided by various agencies. The type of housing provided is normal (predominately self-contained) and is dispersed among mainstream housing blocks in order to achieve a level of normalisation and encourage independent living.

Aims and objectives

The overall aim of the project is to show that extensive social integration is possible even after many years of homelessness, and despite a low capacity for self-help, or a lack of personal prospects.

The objectives of the project are:

- to create normal housing for long-term homeless persons;
- to reduce the number of placements in institutions;
- to provide home-based aftercare services;
- to achieve the institutional separation of housing and support services;
- to encourage cooperation with conventional housing enterprises;
- to promote the principle of independent living.

Innovation

The project is considered innovative because it aims to provide normal housing for people who are long-term homeless and who have serious difficulties in sustaining tenancies.

Inputs

1 Agencies and partnerships

The agencies involved in the project are *Wilhelmsdorf* shelter and two housing companies.

The *Wilhelmsdorf* shelter which cooperates with a housing company owned the conversion projects; the new build project was owned and managed by a housing company. Partnership arrangements exist between *Wilhelmsdorf* and housing companies. Local authorities are involved in the grants for housing construction. There are special agreements between local authorities and social welfare departments on *Länder* level about financing of social support and welfare assistance.

2 Areas and responsibility

Wilhelmsdorf shelter is responsible for the overall management of the project as well as the allocation of tenancies. The housing companies are involved in the construction and management of the housing.

Staff provide support services from *Wilhelmsdorf*. It is intended that 6.5 posts reduce the level of support staffing over a period of five years. If, after that time, aftercare support is still needed, this would be provided by either the city social services or by volunteers.

3 Target groups and numbers

There are two primary target groups:
- long-term homeless men with serious personal and social difficulties for whom 24 flats were created to accommodate a total of 26 homeless persons;
- people who are not homeless for whom a further 26 social rented housing units (flats) are provided.

The target groups are therefore a mix of people who are homeless and those with no particular special needs. This mix allows for normalisation of living environment and is intended to encourage reintegration and, by extension, discourage segregation. In selecting people who are homeless for the project, the focus is on those who have been in a shelter for an extremely long time (13 years on average).

4 Funding

The project has three construction projects, one of which is targeted exclusively at homeless people while the other two cater for homeless as well as non-homeless clients.

The *Gartenhaus* conversion of a former shelter for use by the project cost €695,000. A mixture of institutional capital contribution (old building and land) covered the costs (22.4%), capital market finance (11.5%) and Land and city loans (66.2%).

The project also includes the construction of 25 new flats. The total costs for this element of the project amount to €2.08 million, of which 32% were covered by housing enterprise, 14.4% by institutions, and 52.7% by city and Land loans.

A further 15 flats were also constructed as part of the project. The total costs for these flats were €1.62 million. City and Land loans covered 71.3% of the costs while institutional capital contribution in the form of money and land covered 28.7%.

It can therefore be seen that the overall project costs are shared between three principle sources: city and Land loans, institutional funding to facilitate a move towards community living and capital market finance.

Implementation

1 Services and delivery

Support services are designed to encourage tenants to be independent, to enhance their capacity to manage their own affairs, and to foster social integration. Support services include health, financial, social and enhanced housing management. These are delivered on an individual, client–centred basis.

The support services, which are being delivered by the discharging institution (*Wilhelmsdorf*), will continue until the posts are redesignated after 1999.

2 Accommodation

Part of the original homeless shelter has been converted to create 10 separate housing units. Eight of these are single-person flats while two provide shared accommodation for a total of four people. Through the conversion programme, shelter residents who used to live in highly shared accommodation are now able to benefit from more independent living arrangements under tenancy agreements.

In addition to the conversion programme, two new construction programmes have yielded a total of 40 flats. In the first programme, which was completed in November 1995, 25 flats were built. Of these, nine offer self-contained accommodation for single people. Once again, residents of the former *Wilhelmsdorf* shelter have been accommodated in these new flats. In the second new build programme where 15 flats were completed in July 1997, homeless people are housed in six of the flats.

3 Integration

Social integration is provided through the individualised support package. Part of the integration package is to develop relations between the service users with a long history of homelessness and mainstream tenants sharing the new buildings. These relations appear to be developing in a largely positive direction.

Outputs

1 Monitoring and evaluation

A variety of methods have been used to evaluate the projects. These include tenant as well as social worker surveys. Tenant surveys have been conducted at intervals in two projects. In addition, semi-standardised questionnaires have been distributed to the main project partners. The agency partners' questionnaire considered motivational factors for cooperation, anticipated benefits and drawbacks and implementation problems.

Tenants were considered to be more in command of the respective skills one year after occupation. Tenants indicated that they undertake more activities and frequently have social contacts with people outside the institution. Most tenants felt that their situation had significantly improved. However, overall it is concluded that "only some of the tenants can be described as being largely independent and there may even be an increased need for assistance for some of the tenants after the end of the five-year period".

Support needs changed over time. The health of some tenants had worsened and thus need for nursing care had increased. Time expended on social work declined. Greater support requirements were also reported in relation to leisure time and organisation of daily routines. Similarly, support in dealing with authorities did not decrease over time. While relations between the previously homeless tenants and mainstream neighbours appeared to be developing in a largely positive direction, people sharing the two-person flats experienced difficulties in relation to integration.

2 Problem areas

The status of service users in relation to responsibility for funding is a problem. As residents of the shelter, the homeless men were regarded as 'people without a settled way of living' and funding was therefore the responsibility of the Land. However, as residents of normal housing, they are the responsibility of the social welfare services of the city of Bielefeld. The change in status and responsibility area created a distinction between local and non-local homelessness which threatened to undermine the project.

Second, financing of 'subsequent support' for former residents of a shelter is intended for only a short time whereas this project aimed to rehouse people who would need continuing support to remain independent in the community.

The two two-person flats posed a problem since none of the residents wanted to share. Flats were reclassified as single person after consultation with the funding agency. The new buildings are located in relatively isolated areas which presented problems in terms of integration and the affordability of public transport.

3 Dissemination

The project has been subject to detailed evaluation and the results of the evaluation have been published.

Case study 14

Country:	Greece
Name of project:	*Arsis*
Location:	Athens, Thessaloniki, Volos, Patra, Xanthi and Ioannina
Start date:	1992

Overview

This project provides a range of support services as well as short-term accommodation to young people under the age of 21.

Aims and objectives

The aim of the project is to develop initiatives and organise projects for the provision of social support to young people facing social exclusion and the risk of marginalisation. The objectives of the project are:

- to provide housing for the target group;
- to provide training for the target group;
- to address the overall social and psychological support needs of these individuals in order to achieve an optimum outcome.

Innovation

The project is considered innovative because it addresses the diversity of needs and issues facing young people. These needs include housing, social and psychological support, vocational training, access to employment as well as personal and social development. The recognition of the multi-faceted and complex problems facing socially excluded young people is a real innovation in the Greek context.

Inputs

1 Agencies and partnerships

Arsis is a non-profit organisation. *Arsis* cooperates with a number of agencies in the delivery of its services. These include the Society for the Welfare of Minors, which provides the accommodation, and the *MZ Club Hellas*, which provides the motorcycle engineering training.

2 Areas and responsibility

Arsis is responsible for assessing the needs and suitability of young people admitted to its projects. The organisation takes on all management responsibilities.

3 Target groups and numbers

The project specifically targets young men and women under 21 who are experiencing difficulties in socially integrating, particularly those who are in conflict with the law or who have exhibited failure in social functioning. Within the Greek context, work targeted at this client group is unique since the existing system of statutory service provision largely ignores the needs of this client group. As a voluntary sector organisation, *the principals of free choice and personal responsibility on the part of young people guide Arsis' work.* Among the young people who have so far participated in the projects and activities, approximately 50% are juvenile offenders, 25% face severe social problems in their immediate environment and 80% have experienced some level of difficulty in their family lives.

4 Funding

Arsis obtains funding from various different sources, most of which is for discrete elements of its work. Funding is a major issue for the organisation since continuity of projects is dependent on long-term funding security and several projects have been discontinued or postponed due to termination of funding. The main sources of funding are: subsidies from the EU, subsidies from the General Secretariat for the Young Generation (a department of the Ministry of Education), private offers and donations from individuals, donations from organisations and profit from the carpentry workshop. The guest house accommodation is funded by the Society for the Welfare of Minors, a voluntary organisation which provides the building. The planned catering business is expected to receive funding for the purchase of required equipment and for project operation from statutory sources.

Implementation

1 Services and delivery

Arsis provides the following services: assessment of need; liaison with social services, legal and youth services; organisation of training courses; provision of counselling and support services; organisation of various activities for young people; training of staff and volunteers and the creation of a network of volunteer youth workers. The specific activities organised by *Arsis* are:

- an employment bureau which offers career counselling and advice and acts as a mediator between young people and potential employers;
- vocational training including: carpentry, motorcycle engineering, crafts, arts and culture;
- the Bureau of Central Planning and Administration which provides planning, development, coordination, public and international relations, research, personnel, volunteer training and supervision, legal and financial services;
- guest house accommodation for young homeless people.

2 Accommodation

Arsis provides a guest house for young homeless people aged between 15 and 21 years. The guest house offers temporary accommodation. Providing accommodation for this age group is unique in the Greek context. And the accommodation is in the same building as the Support Centre for Young People which means that residents have access to the diverse services offered by *Arsis*.

The guest house has the capacity to accommodate six young people, but current renovation should increase this number to 10. So far, only young women have been admitted to the guest house although the agency is considering admitting young men as well. Admission is contingent upon obtaining written permission from a parent or legal guardian for those under 18, interview, assessment and the level of interest shown in training and other activities offered. Drug users are specifically excluded from the accommodation since *Arsis* is not equipped to deal with their needs and these people may be disruptive to the functioning of the accommodation. The length of stay in the accommodation ranges from a few days to one year with a usual initial three-month renewable contract pending review.

3 Integration

Arsis runs a number of projects and activities aimed at promoting the social reintegration of young people. These activities which are coordinated by the Support Centre For Young People include: vocational training in carpentry skills (although this aspect of the work has been downsized due to lack of funding); training in motorcycle engineering provided on a cooperative basis with *MZ Club Hellas* (again this has been temporarily discontinued due to lack of funding); various art and cultural activities designed to bring young people into contact with theatre, art, photography, cinema and printing. The aim of the art and cultural activities is to promote personal development and self-confidence. *Arsis'* workshops are dispersed over a wide geographic area. While some training is physically linked to the centre, other courses are more mobile and are offered for short periods in specific locations.

Two further projects are in the planning stages. The first project, which is currently being run by two volunteers who are expected to benefit from part of the profits, is a crafts business. The second project which is awaiting arrival of funding is a catering business.

Outputs

1 Monitoring and evaluation

Since 1992, 200 young people have attended the projects of *Arsis*. Of these, nearly 25% have participated in the vocational training programmes and 10% have found steady employment, 20% have held occasional jobs and 5% have returned to school. There is evidence that young people who have been involved in *Arsis'* projects have made progress in terms of social participation, a change of attitude and increased levels of education.

2 Problem areas

The principal problem area for *Arsis* is access to and security of funding. The pattern of fragmented funding precludes longer-term planning and uses up valuable staff time in chasing various funding sources and options.

A second problem encountered relates to the very nature of the work within the context of Greek society. Because of its innovative approach and philosophy which differs from the mainstream and statutory service provision and also because it is a non-profit organisation, *Arsis* encounters prejudice and suspicion with the result that it spends considerable time and effort establishing itself, educating and proving the importance of its work.

3 Dissemination

Arsis has participated in a number of events including conferences, seminars and forums both in Greece as well as in other European countries. Part of the organisation's activities involves the stimulation of public debate on issues of homelessness and the needs of young people. *Arsis* has established links with other agencies in Greece and beyond.

Case study 15

Country	Greece
Name of project:	*The Athens City Council Centre for the Homeless*
Location:	Athens
Start date:	October 1996

Overview

This project provides temporary shelter for homeless people in Athens. Some support services are also provided at the centre and focus on helping people to find housing and employment.

Aims and objectives

The aims of the project are:
- to address the needs of homeless people in the capital city;
- to provide emergency assistance to homeless people;
- to provide opportunities for reintegration based on assisting individuals and families in crisis in order to enable them to secure housing.

The objectives of the project are to provide a three-phase programme which includes a day care centre, transitory accommodation and, eventually, a reintegration programme focused on labour market reinsertion.

Innovation

The project is considered innovative because it represents the first initiative by a council or local authority in Greece to address the issues of homelessness.

Inputs

1 Agencies and partnerships

Athens City Council. The Homeless Persons Bureau manages the hostel accommodation.

2 Areas of responsibility

The Homeless Persons Bureau is responsible for the administration of the project. Social workers are responsible for gathering information from prospective clients.

3 Target groups and numbers

The day care service caters for approximately 200 people (out of an estimated total of 350 homeless people in Athens). Individuals are admitted to the programme after an assessment by social workers. Clients using the day care service come from diverse educational backgrounds (some with stereotypically low levels of education while others have attended university). There is a wide age range and both men and women appear to use the service. Most service users have held jobs prior to becoming homeless. The temporary accommodation unit is available to a maximum of 104 people. As with the day care service, the hostel is used by both men and women although the number of men is usually higher. There is a wide age range of clients.

The hostel accommodation is open to homeless people who are eligible for a homeless person's card and who have no demanding special needs. Groups excluded are: people requiring personal or nursing care, people with mental illness, ex-offenders with a serious history of crime, people suffering from AIDS (not HIV), people who are drug or alcohol dependent and people who are visiting the capital city. Phase III of the project has to be launched. Information on target groups is not available.

4 Funding

Phases I and II of the project are funded entirely by Athens City Council while Phase III will be funded by the EU.

Implementation
1 Services and delivery

The project consists of three phases. Phase I involved the establishment of a day care centre where meal services, laundry services, personal care and hygiene facilities and medical services were made available. The aim of Phase II is to provide temporary hostel accommodation to residents. Service users are offered a bed, room cleaning services, breakfast as well as counselling and support to enable their reintegration and resettlement. Phase III, which was due to be launched in the beginning of 1998, aims to provide a reintegration programme for people who have been marginalised over a long period of time. Since social housing is critically lacking in Greece, the project will focus on assisting clients to reintegrate into the labour market in order to secure the resources which would enable them to access their own housing.

2 Accommodation

Accommodation is provided through Phase II of the project. The City Council has rented a hotel and converted it for its purposes. Residents usually share rooms with two or three others. The maximum length of stay is six months although, in exceptional cases, this can be extended. The residents' stay in the accommodation is dependent on their compliance with the rules and regulations of the project and their respect for other residents.

3 Integration

Phase III of the project is expected to provide reintegration into the labour market through training and employment, possibly within the project itself. One area of work which is being considered is catering. The possibility of setting up a newspaper to be sold by homeless people is also being investigated.

Outputs

I Monitoring and evaluation

Given the relative newness of the project, realistic evaluation has not been conducted. The fact that the day care centre caters for nearly 60% of Athens' estimated homeless population suggests that the project is reaching its target population.

2 Problem areas

Unknown

3 Dissemination

Unknown.

Case study 16

Country:	Ireland
Name of project:	*Homeless Initiative, Dublin Region*
Location:	Dublin, Wicklow, Kildare
Start date:	1996

Overview

An initiative established in the Dublin region to establish a framework for the coordination of the work of both voluntary agencies and statutory bodies working in the area of homelessness.

Aims and objectives

The aim of the project is to coordinate the responses of statutory and voluntary organisations in providing services for homeless people in the Dublin Region. The focus is on coordinating work between the Eastern Health Board, the Dublin Region local authorities and voluntary organisations.

The objectives of the project are: to initiate research projects which examine the potential of information technology services for homeless people, produce performance indicators and implications for service delivery, identify the effects of an increased number of asylum seekers on homelessness and identify the manner in which effective planning, delivery and coordination of services to the homeless in the Eastern Health Board area can be achieved in the long-term.

Innovation

The project is considered innovative because it proposes the coordination of a comprehensive review of ways to improve delivery of services to homeless people in a large regional area. The emphasis is on planned development and delivery of services which embraces flexibility amid consultation and coordination. This is an unprecedented development in the Irish context in relation to homelessness.

Inputs

1 Agencies and partnerships

The agencies involved are the Eastern Health Board, local authorities, voluntary organisations and the Department of the Environment. The director and the board are comprised of representatives from interested parties. Responsible agencies identified above are involved in the coordination work. Links with independent experts are established for specific research projects.

2 Areas of responsibility

Working groups are established to take responsibility for key areas of work. The key areas of work are: coordination, best practice, research, settlement, outreach and funding. Membership of the working groups extends beyond the board of management.

3 Target groups and numbers

The initiative is not a direct service provider to homeless people. The target group is all organisations providing services for homeless people and those who have the potential to do so.

4 Funding

Funding for the initiative (€761,800) comes from central government, through the Departments of Health (€444,409) and Environment (€317,435).

Implementation

1 Services and delivery

The project is comprised of several different working groups. The Coordination Working Group is responsible for improving knowledge of services, identifying gaps in services and in delivery structures and organisation, improving contact and trust between agencies and promoting a better understanding of partnerships. This is achieved through issue-based fora.

The Partnership Working Group is responsible for organising meetings and programmes to bring together interested and concerned parties with external experts. It is also responsible for the identification of the aims, objectives and potential achievements of partnership working. The Research on Information Technology Working Group is responsible for the review of existing IT usage and the development of recommendations for its enhancement and extension.

The Best Practice Working Group is responsible for developing performance indicators and recommended procedures; raising of consciousness, developing standards of performance for each agency; monitoring.

The Research Working Group is responsible for improving the knowledge base for planning and coordination, identifying shortfalls, developing measures, assessing homelessness, developing the understanding of routes to homelessness, developing a service audit, assessing the use of services, understanding buildings, the costs of services and funding.

The Settlement Working Group, which focuses on an area of prime priority, is responsible for the development of a settlement strategy which would facilitate movement from emergency temporary accommodation to permanent stable and secure accommodation of appropriate standard. This work is undertaken in the context of the current absence of any coordinated strategy for resettlement where homeless people are caught in the vicious cycle of movement between temporary and emergency institutions and rough sleeping and so on.

The Outreach Working Group is responsible for securing a coordinated outreach programme with secure funding. This includes identification of current services offered, identification of gaps in outreach service provision, definition and allocation of responsibilities, development of good practice models through the examination of indigenous and overseas examples and the presentation of future proposals.

The Funding Working Group is responsible for developing a transparent funding regime which covers and dispenses with deficiencies currently apparent, especially with regard to securing support services.

2 Accommodation

The project does not provide any direct services to homeless people.

3 Integration

The project does not provide any direct services to homeless people.

Outputs

1 Monitoring and evaluation

The initiative is currently being evaluated by the Institute of Public Administration.

2 Problem areas

It is too early to identify problem areas in detail. However, there are some general concerns relating to two areas. The first is the absence of 'homelessness' as a statutory concern for national planning and resource allocation. The second area of concern relates to the size of the voluntary sector involved in the provision of housing for homeless people. While the number of housing units provided has increased in actual terms over the recent decades, the number of providers has remained static. Recent funding initiatives by central government are set to maintain the role of existing voluntary sector organisations but are unlikely to provide seed funding for new initiatives or new agencies to become involved in the field. This raises issues of accountability with regard to democratic control over public finance.

3 Dissemination

The findings of the evaluation will be disseminated.

Case study 17

Country:	Italy
Name of project:	*The San Marcellino Association*
Location:	Genoa
Start date:	The parent project began in 1945; the present project began in 1986

Overview

This project provides a range of services to meet the individual needs of people who are severely marginalised and homeless.

Aims and objectives

The aim of the project is to provide diversified services for seriously marginalised people of no abode based on individual case plans.

The objectives of the project are to provide social reinsertion for people of no abode using a variety of resources and instruments in different types of accommodation. This involves the provision of flexible services in three main areas – easy access, advice/reception and rehabilitation.

Innovation

This project is considered innovative because it:
- provides individualised case plans to enable relative integration of seriously marginalised people;
- acts simultaneously on different aspects of the life of the individual;
- coordinates its work with other public and voluntary sector agencies;
- offers flexible solutions including emergency provision and long-term solutions.

Inputs

1 Agencies and partnerships

The principal agency is *San Marcellino* which cooperates with Caritas (*Centro Monastero*) that operates a similar service, the local authority (night) shelter (referrals), CAD (public sector social services for elderly people – rent subsidy), mental health services (joint casework plans) and the local authority Solidarity Office (finance).

A network approach rather than a partnership is in place. The network operates on a division of labour approach assuming that other types of services are locally available and provided. However, a genuine networking approach has yet to be realised.

2 Areas of responsibility

San Marcellino is structured on the basis of internal sections with distinct management units – the advice section, the easy access services and the rehabilitation services. Each is evaluated separately and staff and volunteers are drawn from different sources and training routes.

The Technical Operational Group for the project aims to establish responsibilities and find common methods of working. It consists of representatives from the district social services offices, the municipal shelter, *San Marcellino* and *Caritas*.

3 Target groups and numbers

The target group is the *senza dimora*, or people of 'no abode'. Within this broad target group, there are distinct categories catered for by the three service areas. A total of 746 people annually attend the Advice Centre (80% male, average age 49). Of this total, 63% are homeless people, 29% are people with mental health problems, 42% are people with alcohol or drug problems, 17% are people leaving prison and 9% are disabled people. Some people have multiple problems. Approximately 80 people are 'given hospitality' in reintegration projects. Thirty-five people are housed in protected housing.

4 Funding

As a voluntary agency, *San Marcellino* relies on voluntary workers to reduce costs. A total of 40% of total costs are paid for by local authorities, mainly the municipality, and mainly in terms of rent support. The remainder is raised through voluntary and private donations.

Implementation

1 Services and delivery

The three main services are described below. The Advice Centre (the oldest of the services) has assumed an increasingly central role, becoming the place where cases are selected and managed (that is, the referral system onto other external services or to internal services). This involves a willingness to participate, social work assessment and a long-term individual reintegration plan.

Easy Access Services include social activities, surgery and pharmacy and a clothing store.

Rehabilitation Services include : health (for example, alcohol treatment centre), work (protected workshops and work reinsertion), socialisation (recreation centre) and accommodation (shelters, transitional or supported accommodation and protected housing). The rehabilitation project is described as "a pilot project that is continually changing in an effort to adapt to changing realities of (people)". The casework rehabilitation plan includes housing, employment, training and social support needs.

Access to services, other than the easy access services, is dependent on selection, managed by the Advice Centre, and the establishment of a meaningful relationship with the social worker.

2 Accommodation

The accommodation offered represents a fundamental pillar around which other aspects of a care plan revolve. The housing reintegration plan is no longer seen as a ladder.

There are two night shelters offering 16 and 13 places respectively. Shelter accommodation is a response to housing emergency and represents a break from street life. At the shelters, the aim is to instil a new life-style in the individual. Stays at the shelters are intended for a period of three months but are generally longer in practice.

The project operates Protected Communities which are seen as an intermediate facility with the potential for subsequent admission to proper accommodation. Users of the Protected Communities participate in the running of the community where the aim is the promotion of socialisation and the development of necessary capacities for access to proper accommodation. The Protected Communities house a maximum of eight people with a minimum stay of one year. The Protected Hostel arose from the recognition that some people would not develop skills required to independently manage proper accommodation. The Protected Hostel is intended for those who require support. The objective is maintenance rather than rehabilitation.

Protected (proper) housing is not seen as a solution in itself but as an instrument to monitor the level of meaningful relationships formed. A total of 22 spaces are available in protected (proper) housing. This type of housing ranges from one-person apartments to three-bedroom apartments to larger apartments divided to accommodate four individuals. Individuals are allocated the accommodation with a 'for non-living use' contract. This means that they cannot give the address as their official place of residence.

3 Integration

The reintegration/rehabilitation work focuses on the individualised care plan with long-term options for work. This is a departure from the more normal short-term or emergency work offered. Socialisation and work training are also included within the reintegration work. User participation in the operation of the community dwellings also forms part of the support package. Thus, *San Marcellino* offers a range of support and reintegration services which recognise the multi-dimensional needs of its target group. However, reintegration is seen as relative to the seriousness of the needs of the individual since the target group is people who are severely marginalised.

Outputs

1 Monitoring and evaluation

A very formal and systematic structure of monitoring is in place. This includes individual case assessment and general assessment of the activities. The assessment of general activities takes the form of an annual review when the Centre closes for one week and the manager and volunteers for each sector carry out a review and report to the Study Group. This Group consists of the president of the association, the psychologist and managers of the main sectors. The Study Group reports to the Management Committee.

2 Problem areas

There is reference to the fact that, since all those in the accommodation projects are receiving public sector support, "of inducing, of piloting certain things towards those who have the resources or those who are entitled to public sector finance".

3 Dissemination

There is reference to the report from the study group to the management committee. Also it "promotes meetings and exchange of information between public and private sector organisations operating in the no abode field".

Case study 18

Country:	Luxembourg
Name of project:	*Wunnengshellef*
Location:	Country-wide
Start date:	1988

Overview

This project, which is based on a strong partnership, provides long-term housing and an individualised social integration and insertion package to homeless people.

Aims and objectives

The aims of the project are:
* to create a social integration and reinsertion programme for vulnerable people;
* to facilitate access to suitable housing in good condition on a long-term basis;
* to raise awareness and sensitise politicians, the public and private sector to the issues of homelessness.

The objectives of the project are:
* to identify suitable housing for people leaving reception centres and to house them accordingly on a long-term although not permanent basis;
* to provide each resident with a socio–educational support programme to meet their needs;
* to work in partnership with a range of associations and reception centres who act as referring agencies and who are charged with the direct provision of social support services;
* to liaise with landlords in the public and private sectors in order to negotiate tenancies which are then sub-let to clients.

Innovation

Wunnengshellef is the only project in Luxembourg which provides long-term accommodation (not permanent). The project is also considered innovative in the following areas:

- financial assessment of the individual based on household resources rather than market requirements;
- cooperative working between similar initiatives to arrive at common solutions for the provision of housing;
- each service user is provided with a written contract detailing a personalised social accompaniment programme and service users are obliged to accept support;
- involvement of private landlords as active partners in the project;
- housing is seen as an integral element of reinsertion work and is placed on the same footing as social reintegration;
- the project is not a direct service provider to homeless people but rather a service to other associations.

Inputs

I Agencies and partnerships

The following agencies were the founders of the organisation: *Maison de la Porte Ouverte, Jongenheem, Caritas, Fondation du Tricentenaire, Action Sociale pour Jeunes* and *Entente des Gestionnaires des Centres d'Accueil.*

Wunnengshellef is an association of associations. By definition, it works with its member associations. As of March 1997, the project included 21 partners whose activities include:

- housing, reception and accompaniment work with children;
- advice and information for pregnant women;
- work with families;
- social reintegration of homeless people;
- social, cultural and professional insertion of young unemployed;
- outreach work with young people leaving foyers;
- training and employment for women in distress;
- social guidance, information and advice regarding household management;
- support and housing for single-parent families;
- respite care for families caring for people with physical disabilities;

- day time and night time reception for women;
- support for people with mental illness;
- advice, information and emergency housing for women experiencing domestic violence;
- prevention, ambulatory services, reintegration and substitution services for drug users.

Project partners contribute effectively in two ways:
- the selection and referral of clients to *Wunnengshellef*;
- the provision of social support services to clients once they are placed in *Wunnengshellef* accommodation. The nature of support services varies according to each individual's needs as well as the mandate and methods of working of each service provider. There is little attempt to coordinate the support services provided.

2 Areas of responsibility

Wunnengshellef is responsible for:
- identifying, purchasing or renting suitable accommodation;
- assessing the individual's suitability for the project;
- collecting from the individual a rental payment according to their means;
- liaising with the landlord.

Wunnengshellef has a fivefold structure. The management is responsible for the daily administration of the project including identification of property, negotiation, housing management. *Le Comité Restreint* has a consultative role within the project. The Administrative Council which meets bi-annually is responsible for ratifying any strategic changes to the project and for overseeing the project as a whole. The Management Committee is similar in role to the Administrative Council but includes within its membership a representative of the Ministry of the Family. The Pilot Group which was established to consider innovation within the project has not functioned effectively due to lack of interest from partners.

3 Target groups and numbers

Priority is given to persons referred by member organisations. Target groups are widely varied and reflect the membership of the project.

These include single parents, homeless people, people with mental illness, drug/alcohol users, people with physical disabilities, women experiencing domestic violence, young people, unemployed people and children.

4 Funding

The project is dependent on two principal sources of funding:
- funding from the Ministry of the Family which initially commissioned the project;
- funds raised through its own income-generating activities. Instead of rent, tenants pay a usage indemnity. As the holdings of the project have increased since its inauguration in 1988, so, too, its income from its activities as well as its fixed assets have grown.

Implementation

1 Services and delivery

Wunnengshellef's principal activities are: the identification and acquisition of appropriate accommodation, renovation of properties as necessary and facilitation of access to the property for referred households. Properties are usually either purchased outright or rented from the private sector, although some properties are also acquired from the public sector (usually at no cost).

Once habitable, the property is placed at the disposal of families or individuals in need who are referred to the project by member associations and whom *Wunnengshellef* assesses. The project then acts as the principal tenant, sub-letting the property to the residents and thus ensuring the landlord of a guaranteed rental income as well as good housing management.

Where renovation work is required to render the property habitable, it is usually carried out by potential residents who may be long-term unemployed under the supervision of an experienced builder. The training and work programme forms an integral part of the reintegration objectives of the project and enables residents to take responsibility for their housing as well as helping them to develop marketable skills. The condition of the property and the work required to render it habitable may influence the tenancy arrangements in favour of the project, such that a lower rent is negotiated.

All residents living in *Wunnengshellef* properties are required to accept a support programme provided or organised by the referring agency. *Wunnengshellef* usually provides housing management support itself. One element of housing management support involves raising the residents' awareness of potential problems in the home through a visual *aide memoire* which empowers them to identify any problems and report them quickly.

2 Accommodation

In 1988, the project began with three units of accommodation. As of 1996, the project held 122 units of accommodation. The majority of the housing provided is in flats, either one, two or three bedrooms. In general, the maximum stay allowable in a *Wunnengshellef* property is three years, although 37% of clients have stayed beyond the three-year limit.

3 Integration

Reintegration is based on the double axis of stability in housing and social accompaniment to re-establish community links, develop self-confidence and meet the specific needs of the diverse client group. In addition, reintegration through housing management support is provided. Depending on the needs of the client, labour market reintegration may also form an element of the support programme provided either through *Wunnengshellef's* own activities (renovation, etc) or through the referring agency.

Outputs

1 Monitoring and evaluation

The project was subject to an evaluation in 1994 with the following findings:

- 56% of service users considered that *Wunnengshellef* played a significant role in bringing about changes to their daily lives;
- autonomy, independence, dignity and responsibility were the most frequently mentioned benefits of the project;
- the success of the labour market integration appears to be limited with few service users seeing direct benefits and few gaining employment;

- access to housing helped service users to re-establish ties with family and friends and to build new relationships;
- half the service users experienced improvement in their financial position, the other half experienced deterioration;
- since its conception, *Wunnengshellef* has had 639 requests for housing; the number of units held has grown steadily but tailed off in 1996 due to a shortage of available units and a sizeable turnover of residents in that year;
- the project appears to have had a growing impact in the political arena as evidenced by its regular participation in a number of political fora. The project is often used as a point of reference by the relevant ministries and public sector housing has been put at its disposal at no cost. However, the project has yet to succeed in its efforts to bring about concrete change in legislation or measures to alleviate the difficulties experienced by vulnerable people in relation to housing.

2 Problem areas

Unknown.

3 Dissemination

Wunnengshellef organises a number of activities to publicise its work and to sensitise politicians to the issues of housing. These include: official inaugurations of new properties which are attended by the media, targeted, issue-specific demonstrations, information dissemination through stands and brochures as well as round table discussions.

Case study 19

Country:	The Netherlands
Name of project:	*The Social Recovery Project*
Location:	The Hague
Start date:	Not known

Overview

Different services, housing associations and the municipality work together on a local basis to provide integrated services for the homeless. Under the government initiative following the 1994 Welfare Act, The Hague brought forward a project to prevent social exclusion for homeless, addicts, ex-offenders, young homeless and ex-psychiatric patients. National government required the municipalities to bring forward proposals for projects aimed at innovative policies in the social and cultural fields.

Aims and objectives

The aims of the project are:
• to clarify the division of responsibilities between national and local government after the 1994 Welfare Act; under this Act the government is responsible for stimulating new policies and innovative projects;
• to integrate different sectors of welfare work.

Innovation

This initiative is considered innovative because it aims to integrate policies concerning housing, welfare and work. Several projects emerged: *Maatschappelijk Herstel (MH)* – housing focus; *Zorgdakcontract* – contract between housing and care agencies provides coaching towards independence for people formerly in institutions. Five housing associations work together with a whole range of service providers.

Inputs

1 Agencies and partnerships

The principal agencies are the municipal authority, welfare organisations and five housing associations.

2 Areas of responsibility

The municipal authority established a project office with staff from different sectors. The welfare organisations proposed projects.

3 Target groups and numbers

The projects target single people only. During the first year, 1996, 40 houses with 120 rooms were available. After two years, 400 houses are available each year in the housing pool for service providers to draw upon.

4 Funding

A total of €3,630,240 (8 million guilders) 1994-98.

Implementation

1 Services and delivery

The emphasis is on the provision of small permanent housing. *Maatschappelijk Herstel* (*MH*) – housing focus. *Zorgdakcontract* offers a housing and care contract. Service providers came together in five different clusters: mental health, youth help, addiction, ex-offender rehabilitation, general welfare.

2 Accommodation

Housing associations make housing available under the ABC model (that is, lease to service providers who let to clients). In The Hague project, a pool of houses was introduced and central access was available for service providers to find accommodation the *Maatschappelijk Herstel* (*MH*). Service providers rent accommodation for six months, renewable for an additional maximum of six months.

3 Integration

The aim is to enable people dependent on services to learn to live independently in one year after which time they gain access to normal social housing from one of the housing associations involved in the project. Only 10% of the available stock may be in use for clients who are no longer receiving support.

Outputs

1 Monitoring and evaluation

The service providers make most of the effort, while housing associations run few risks. Of a target population of some 10,000 almost 1,000 were reached through the various projects. Municipal authorities have learned about social welfare projects through involvement with partnership agencies.

2 Problem areas

"In almost all Maatschappelijk Herstel projects a problem is posed by the outflow of clients into normal life" and ways are being considered to improve this part of the process. Extension to include ambulatory services poses a problem because service providers are not financed that way. An extension of the *Zorgdakcontract* with housing associations to deal with anti-social behaviour and evictions is being considered.

3 Dissemination

Unknown.

Case study 20

Country:	The Netherlands
Name of project:	*Walenburg*
Location:	Amsterdam
Start date:	Not known

Overview

Walenburg is a step–model project. It offers clients the chance to move up and/or down the housing ladder from supported to more independent housing.

Aims and objectives

The project aims to enable people to choose housing and support to meet their individual needs.

Innovation

The project is considered innovative because it offers the flexibility to move up and down the ladder of care by providing a chain of housing options from sheltered to independent living.

Inputs

1 Agencies and partnerships

The main agencies are the municipal housing association and *Walenburg*.

2 Areas of responsibility

The Housing Association is responsible for housing; *Walenburg* is responsible for support.

3 Target groups and numbers

The project targets single homeless men exclusively.

4 Funding

Unknown.

Implementation

1 Services and delivery

Unknown.

2 Accommodation

The accommodation is divided into a four-stepped system. In Step I, clients are offered accommodation in a 60-bed shelter. In Step II, the clients can move to apartments within the shelter. Step III clients move on to 37 small apartments in two independent buildings but continue to share meals at the shelter. Finally, Step IV involves independent living with minimal support.

3 Integration

Unknown.

Outputs

1 Monitoring and evaluation

A total of 42 people moved within the project; 26 climbed up and 16 climbed down the ladder.

2 Problem areas

Unknown.

3 Dissemination

Unknown.

Case study 21

Country:	Portugal
Name of project:	*Lisbon Homelessness Project*
Location:	Lisbon
Start date:	November 1997

Overview

This project offers transitional and flexible sheltered accommodation and includes support services. The project came about as a result of EU Poverty III funding.

Aims and objectives

The objectives of the projects are:
- to provide social insertion for homeless people;
- to provide a transitory and flexible shelter to facilitate rehabilitation;
- to provide advice and guidance on homelessness to relevant institutions.

Innovation

The project is considered innovative within the Portuguese context because it offers shelter to homeless people along with a personalised support package.

Inputs

1 Agencies and partnerships

The following agencies are involved: the Municipality of Lisbon, *Assistencia Medica Internacional* (Foundation of International Medical Assistance – *AMI*), *O Companheiro* (Association of Christian Fraternity).

2 Areas of responsibility

The Municipality of Lisbon has adapted one of its buildings to provide a night shelter. The municipality also provides technical assistance to

AMI as well as financial support to cover the maintenance of the shelter. *AMI* manages the shelter and provides an integration programme based on counselling and personal skills.

O *Comanheiro* has adapted the building. O *Comanheiro* also assesses clients for job training (civil/construction) and assists them in integrating in the areas of work.

3 Target groups and numbers

The project targets homeless men aged 18–65 who have no history of mental illness. The maximum capacity is for 27 individuals (currently 17 people involved).

4 Funding

The municipality covers running expenses.

Implementation

1 Services and delivery

Clients sign a contract on admission. Clients are referred by social workers from the *AMI* network of centres. The normal length of stay is two months which may be extended if individual circumstances require. The approach is individualised assessment and assistance.

2 Accommodation

Night shelter.

3 Integration

AMI has an employment club which gives assistance in finding employment. Employment and stability of life–style are seen as the cornerstones of the reintegration process. The strategy is based on the use of all the available services in the city.

The project attaches great importance to the role of the family in the reintegration of the individual.

Outputs

1 Monitoring and evaluation

There is a project evaluation committee comprised of representatives of the municipality *AMI*.

2 Problem areas

Unknown.

3 Dissemination

Unknown.

Case study 22

Country:	Spain
Name of project:	*San Martin de Porres*
Location:	Madrid
Start date:	Not known

Overview

This project offers short- and medium-term accommodation and support services to homeless people. Reintegration services are focused on accessing employment and individual housing. The project operates one shelter and a stepping stones accommodation unit which is designed to develop the individual's capacity to sustain a tenancy.

Aims and objectives

The aim of the project is to implement service delivery for emergency and longer-term resettlement and provide solutions which explicitly involve consideration and attention to employment.

Innovation

The project is considered innovative because it focuses on integration especially with regard to occupational training and residential provision.

Inputs

1 Agencies and partnerships

The project is operated by the Dominican Religious Order which works with NGOs, the private sector and the municipality.

2 Areas of responsibilities

Unknown.

3 Target groups and numbers

The project favours admission of those with the greatest potential for resettlement. It offers 72 spaces.

4 Funding

European Community Horizon I and II funds are used for expanding professional training.

Implementation

1 Services and delivery

The project provides shelter for 72 persons with no limit on the duration of stay. The service is open from 6 pm to 9 am. There are differentiated levels of access to the facilities on offer. People showing inclination to self-help, for example, in seeking employment, are granted access to all facilities while those who show limited inclinations have more restricted access. The facilities include an occupational workshop, professional training, integration services, residential integration and a mini-residence and centre of citizenship. Six full-time workers in a binding workshop catering for local demands and supplying external companies provide professional training. Integration services provide advice on employment and assistance in securing jobs for those who are motivated. Once employment is secured, advisers maintain contact with the individual as part of outreach support. Residential integration involves supporting residents to find flats. The mini-residence and Centre of Citizenship is an intermediary position between shelter and self-contained accommodation where independent living can be practised. It takes the form of communal flatted accommodation for 15 persons who take some responsibility for rent payments and the organisation of routines. The Citizenship Centre is used for everyday private activities such as newspaper reading, telephone calls and so on.

2 Accommodation

The project offers 72 places in a shelter and 15 places in the mini-centre.

3 Integration

The focus of integration is on occupational and residential support to enable individuals to find and sustain jobs and self-contained housing. There is a limited aftercare outreach programme.

Outputs

I Monitoring and evaluation

Unknown.

2 Problem areas

Unknown.

3 Dissemination

Unknown.

Case study 23

Country:	Spain
Name of project:	*Zaragoza City – Multiple Projects* (including the municipal shelter, the '*Coordinadora de Transseuntes de Zaragoza*', the *Caritas* reception centre and the Centre for Integration: '*Torre Virreina*' managed by Caritas)
Location:	Zaragoza
Start date:	Various dates
	Latest development Coordinadora – 1989

Overview

This is not a single project but rather a network of different local initiatives.

Aims and objectives

The aim of *Caritas* reception is to provide information for new arrivals in the city, including refugees. The aim of the municipal shelter is to provide a temporary shelter and resettlement programme for the homeless. The *Coordinadora* is an umbrella organisation for five charities whose aim is to coordinate action with public authorities to provide for chronic homeless in the city. The Centre for Integration (*Torre Virreina*) which is managed by *Caritas* aims to promote independent living.

Innovation

Coordinadora is the first attempt at NGO and municipal coordination on homelessness. It is an attempt to establish an example of a well coordinated and integrated system for service delivery to homeless people at the municipal level. The operation of several agencies, each with explicit objectives, in one city is itself an innovation. The limited amount of cooperation and coordination between them is also novel.

Inputs

1 Agencies and partnerships

The project involves NGOs and the municipal authority. The municipal shelter and the Caritas shelter operate without partnerships. *Coordinadora de Transseuntes de Zaragoza* is the umbrella organisation for five NGOs concerned with homelessness in Zaragoza. Their work focuses on the chronically homeless – those who slip through the net of existing provision.

2 Areas of responsibility

The reception centre provides information for new arrivals and refers them to the municipal shelter for short stay – six days maximum. The municipal shelter provides temporary shelter and a resettlement programme for the homeless. The *Coordinadora* is an umbrella organisation responsible for coordinating action with public authorities to provide for chronically homeless people in the city. The Centre for Integration (*Torre Virreina*) offers 22 spaces promoting independent living.

3 Target groups and numbers

The *Coordinadora* focuses on the chronically homeless; the Information Centre targets new arrivals and refugees.

4 Funding

Unknown.

Implementation

1 Services and delivery

The *Coordinadora* provides services to approximately 20 elderly people. A team of volunteers conducted a street search for these chronically homeless people and compiled a dossier on their life-styles and routines.

The individuals were then offered housing in 'La Casa Abierta' – a 'no requirements' centre managed by the municipality.

The reception centre provides information on orientation and services reflecting the needs and interests of the new arrivals. A database is kept on all arrivals which provides information on demand for services.

The municipal shelter offers short-stay accommodation (basic provision of bed and board) for new arrivals and city homeless. It favours those who 'help themselves' by allowing longer stay for those who find a job. There is also special flatted accommodation set aside for people with alcohol problems who are helped through a work group. This programme is linked to others which provide training in social skills and occupational training with private enterprise placements in workplaces.

The Centre for Integration (*Torre Virreina*) organises a three-stepped process of integration: in Step One, clients acquire basic social and hygiene skills, learn to take care of themselves, learn to live alongside others and develop self-esteem and motivation. In this step, the only income that individuals have is a daily allowance. The service includes daily cleaning activities, individual pursuits, self-help group sessions, social skills workshop, occupational activities for acquisition of minimum work habits – for example, building maintenance, gardening etc, free time workshop activities, cultural activities and general learning. During the last three to four months of this stage, residents receive induction and preparation for movement to the next phase. The induction programme includes motivating residents to move to independent living and the preparation of a personal plan for achieving integration.

Step Two is known as 'take off' and lasts between six to eight months. This stage has a total capacity of eight people. It is the central plank of the integration process. This step involves the development of personal plans introducing external activities:

• training activities through professional institutes;
• occupational activities;
• activities involving relationships with other people inside and outside the Centre;
• problem solving, therapy sessions.

Step Three is known as 'exit' and has a maximum duration of three months to avoid dependency. This step includes preparation for leaving the centre and entering the outside world on their own; self-management of personal activities and job seeking as well as continuation of many of the activities in Step Two. A subsidised flat is provided and is attached to the centre. It has the capacity to house five people. With the help of the Parish, a flat is eventually found and the resident of the Centre is relocated.

2 Accommodation

The Centre for Integration provides accommodation for 22 people. The flats in the final stage accommodate five people at a time.

3 Integration

For *Coordinadora*, resettlement and reintegration are beyond the ability of many of the attendees. Therefore, the focus is on smaller objectives – time control, self-esteem, control and regulation of own lives. See details of the Integration Centre under Service delivery.

Outputs

1 Monitoring and evaluation

Unknown.

2 Problem areas

Unknown.

3 Dissemination

Unknown.

Case study 24

Country:	Sweden
Name of project:	*Staircase of Transition*
Location:	National – Stockholm and Gothenburg
Start date:	Evolved in 1980s – established by 1990 in most local authorities

Overview

The concept is of a staircase whereby housing condition standards, security and responsibilities increase incrementally and cumulatively while the amount of support and services is gradually eroded. The final step towards reintegration would be achieved when tenants get their own leasehold flat or house. The length of time spent at different levels varies, but there is an assumption that it will take a few years to climb the staircase.

The *Staircase of Transition* has emerged and spread among many local authorities. Central government has partially adjusted national legislation to reflect the staircase model. The model is used in many municipalities but it is not established on a national level. Local variations may mean that different localities have differently constructed staircases with the number and type of rungs demonstrating great variation and locally specific characteristics.

Aims and objectives

The aim of the project is to provide a staircase to reintegrate homeless people into the regular housing market.

Innovation

Special contracts for staircase improvement of housing – category and training housing had earlier origins, the provision of transitional contract to complement the two preceding steps was established historically through 1970s and 1980s. These three steps – category, training and transitional contract – identify the most common form (model) of the staircase progressive sequence.

Inputs

1 Agencies and partnerships

The key agencies are the local housing authority, the local social authority, the municipal housing companies and private landlords. Most municipalities have only one municipal housing company which is by far the biggest landlord in the area. Public, voluntary and private organisations are also involved.

2 Areas of responsibility

The local authorities rent and sub-let properties from the municipal housing companies as well as private landlords. The local social authorities are responsible for the delivery of services in the transition process.

3 Target groups and numbers

Each step has a specific target group. Step-specific target groups can sometimes be defined in such a way as to make it impossible to move to the next step. The target group for category houses is older single men with alcohol problems and/or mental problems. Although residents of category housing are not theoretically excluded from higher steps on the staircase, in practice exclusion often occurs either because they have not sufficiently reformed or because the property owner does not accept them as tenants. The target group for training houses is people who have successfully participated in treatment programmes for substance abuse. The target group for transitional contract is families with children who have been evicted or rejected because of debts or rent arrears. Besides those living in housing for elderly people and asylum seekers, it is probable that 8,000 households are tenants on special terms with the local social authorities.

4 Funding

Unknown.

Implementation

1 Services and delivery

Characteristically, local social authorities rent the homes and sub-let the properties to clients on special terms. The staircase model operates in many but not all local authorities. The size of the project is determined by each local authority's housing policy. A typical model has three steps:

Step One: category houses and group homes – small flats often of low standard.

Step Two: training flats – sometimes ordinary dwellings, furnished and located near institutions. Staff in a neighbouring institution sometimes monitor these. These flats are rented out furnished. The length of stay is sometimes limited to ensure access by others. The flats do not offer leasehold agreements.

Step Three: transitional contracts – spread out in ordinary residential areas. Tenants are responsible for their own furniture.

Tenants are charged full rent at all stages.

2 Accommodation

There are no recent figures on the size of the staircase model housing. However, it is estimated that over 8,000 housing units are being offered.

3 Integration

The aim of the *Staircase* is to allow progressive movement up the ladder until full integration is achieved through improvement in standards, security of tenure and independent living. (See problems below.)

Outputs

1 Monitoring and evaluation

The staircase model is subject to periodic surveys and local authority review. However, the model has not been the subject of evaluation on a national scale.

2 Problem areas

- The *Staircase* has created a 'secondary housing market' which acts as a down pathway from normal housing to homelessness as much as an up pathway from the street to normal housing. This occurs, typically, when a family falls into arrears or debt and the municipality as an alternative to eviction takes on their household leases.
- The overall outcome of the model is disappointing. Tenants with special contracts often do not reach the 'floor' for renting their own housing. Instead, they may get stuck on the staircase.
- Referral to lower steps is a common sanction for misbehaviour.
- A growing number of housing clients are being labelled as incapable of independent living and are thus excluded from the secondary housing market.

3 Dissemination

Models for support, services and control are locally designed and often disseminated through the media, conferences and/or contact between local authorities.

Case study 25

Country:	United Kingdom
Name of project:	*Neville House*
Location:	London (near Victoria train station)
Start date:	1992/93

Aims and objectives

The aims of the project are:

- to provide temporary winter accommodation for rough sleepers with multiple problems (heavy drinkers and drug abusers, especially poly users);
- to make an impact on local area (Victoria, London);
- to provide a gateway to more permanent support and services.

Innovation

The project is considered innovative because:

- it takes an holistic view of multiple needs of residents;
- is non-judgemental and tolerates failure;
- adopts a flexible, multi-disciplinary approach;
- recognises residents as having multiple skills and interests and tries to provide for these;
- provides a one-stop site for health – mental and physical – needs;
- offers continuity of contact with a key worker.

Inputs

1 Agencies and partnerships

The project is a 'subsidiary' of the permanent St Mungo's charity. The direct provider is St Mungo's Voluntary Organisation. The NGO works with local and central state authorities, a variety of voluntary agencies providing support services, for example, 'Drinks Crisis Centre' running a detoxification unit, counselling services, psychiatric care, private caterers, police liaison and a local residents' committee.

A key feature of this programme is the integration of services for on-site provision. This integration is facilitated through one source funding being the Rough Sleepers Initiative.

2 Responsibilities

St Mungo's provides the guiding hand and full-time workers in the project have day-to-day responsibility.

3 Target groups and numbers

The primary target group is heavy drinkers and drug abusers – especially poly users. The project is designed for rough sleepers in the Victoria area of London. There are 69 bedspaces in shared two/four rooms. Separate accommodation for women is available and there is a detoxification unit. There are both wet and dry areas. The project is open from 1 December to 31 March. During 1996/97 the project housed 348 residents – 79% males, the average age was 36 years, 94% residents were rough sleepers, 78% referred by outreach.

4 Funding

The project is funded under the 'London Winter Shelter Programme' (RSI) from the Department of the Environment. Funding is annually renewed.

Implementation

I Services and delivery

The project offers:
- detoxification if wanted by residents; there is no pressure to take up this service and residents are not evicted if they fail;
- counselling;
- healthcare – physical and psychiatric;
- creative outlets – newsletter, vocational guidance, screen and t-shirt printing, information technology computer outlets, music, photography, artist in residence, craft room and resource centre;
- resettlement assessment with at minimum an attachment to a support worker for aftercare.

2 Accommodation

Neville House provides short-term winter accommodation. The average stay was 21 days although 42% stay less than a week.

3 Integration

The project adopts a flexible and multi-disciplinary approach to meet the variable needs of its residents. The fact that many clients stay only for a short time means that there is little opportunity to arrange for longer-term residence although attempts are made at needs assessment. A key support worker is provided as is a resettlement plan. A total of 5% of residents are permanently resettled (8% was target) and 37% were temporarily resettled (36% was the target).

Outputs

1 Monitoring and evaluation

Funders set evaluation and performance targets. These have nearly been reached. The project's primary achievement is its one-stop approach.

2 Problem areas

Unknown.

3 Dissemination

The ideas on nurturing interests and skills have been picked up elsewhere. The lessons learned from the work include the importance of agency working, funding programmes, tolerance and non-judgemental approach.

Case study 26

Country:	United Kingdom
Name of project:	*Wernham House*
Location:	Aberdeen
Start date:	Around 1987

Overview

This project is a long-term wet hostel for people with severe alcohol abuse and/or mental health problems. The focus is on empowerment and acceptance of responsibility rather than treatment and cure. The project is part of a network of supported accommodation for people with multiple problems.

Aims and objectives

The aim of the project is to remove people from the spiral/cyclical round of institutionalisation while providing a supportive, secure and safe environment for maximisation of independence and self-esteem.

Innovation

The project is considered innovative because it addresses the multiple needs of seriously marginalised people. The project challenges traditional notions of the desirability of resettlement as a measure of success.

Inputs

1 Agencies and partnerships

The project is managed by Aberdeen Cyrenians. It is registered with the social work department which establishes and inspects levels of care. Due to registration, housing benefit is not payable. Instead, a residential allowance per resident is paid such that residents have no bills to pay directly. Thus, in some ways, residents are dependent.

The project provides accommodation and links with social work services. It also links to the housing department for resettlement as well as to the health board and other voluntary agencies for support.

2 Areas of responsibility

Unknown.

3 Target groups and numbers

The target group is people with severe alcohol/mental health problems who are heavily institutionalised. The project supports people with multiple needs who are not dealt with by traditional services.

4 Funding

The project is funded by the local authority social work department on a block basis – that is, global costings – rather than individual needs assessment. This type of funding creates security for the service provider since a vacancy does not result in reduction of income.

Implementation

1 Services and delivery

See 'Integration' below. There is a high staff–resident ratio with 14 staff members offering 24-hour cover.

2 Accommodation

The project accommodates 18 men and women and can cater for couples. Over a 10-year period, between 50 and 60 people have been resident. Each resident has their own lockable room and shares communal areas and communal services. There is no limit on the length of stay.

3 Integration

Residents are difficult to resettle. *Wernham House* is their community where friends locate and it is a familiar place. The project questions the desirability of a permanent tenancy as an indicator of resettlement and integration. The project takes a relaxed view of the process and its desirability. Where residents show an inclination to resettle, they are given every encouragement to do so without pressure. Resettlement candidates are provided with a support worker from Aberdeen Cyrenian staff. Only six residents have moved on to tenancies of their own and these have been successful.

Residents regard *Wernham House* as their home. Residents are encouraged to take maximum personal responsibility at a comfortable pace. Independence is encouraged and self-esteem built up. Residents are encouraged to personalise their rooms – choose their own linen, decorate, have their own TV (communal one provided), eat in their own rooms. There are no set times for communal meals. Residents can bring drink and friends into the hostel. It has been found that residents can address their problems with advice and support. Residents do not have a tenancy though they have been asked whether they want one. Technically they have an occupancy agreement which allows for easier eviction. In reality, only one resident has been evicted in 10 years of operation.

The ethos is that of an accepting regime, creating an atmosphere of security and keeping rules to a minimum. Residents have house meetings and also meet with their key workers. At both meetings, they are encouraged to suggest changes in rules and the operation of the hostel.

Outputs

1 Monitoring and evaluation

The project is evaluated in terms of the level of control residents have been able to take over their lives and the reduction or cessation of their drinking rather than in terms of resettlement. On this basis, *Wernham House* is seen as a success. Few residents have returned to short-stay hostels or rough sleeping. The project continues to operate after 10 years and provides a model for schemes elsewhere.

2 Problem areas

Unknown.

3 Dissemination

Unknown.

Index

and social exclusion 18-21, 23,
30, 39, 47
see also rental sector; social
housing; 'supported housing'

I

Inigo project, Austria 90, 92, 127-30
innovative services for homeless 1-
2, 6, 10-11, 21-4
agency *see* agency services
building programmes 166, 173,
174
case studies 6, 84-97, 122-223
conceptual framework 53
'continuum of care' approach
103-5, 114
contractual approach 100, 101-2,
107, 114, 194
definition 1
development of 83, 84
evaluation and monitoring 85,
100, 102-3, 111, 114, 115-16
appropriateness of targets 66-7
case study schemes 129, 137,
141-2, 153, 168, 174-5, 179,
191, 197-8, 223
flexibility of service 85, 94-7,
100, 113, 114, 184, 204
Italy 95-6, 188-92
Netherlands 103-4, 202-3
'step-models' 103-4, 104-5,
181-3, 202-3, 212-13, 214-17
United Kingdom 96, 218
funding mechanisms 84, 92-4, 95,
112
for pilot programmes 64-7
Austria 92, 125, 128
Belgium 133, 136, 140
Denmark 144-5, 146
Finland 148, 152
France 156, 160, 163
Germany 93, 167, 173
Greece 177, 179, 182
Ireland 185, 186
Italy 93, 189-90
Luxembourg 196
Netherlands 200

Spain 208
United Kingdom 219, 222
individualised approach 105-7, 114,
174, 188-92
institutional framework 59-61, 83,
87, 94
integration of services 70-3, 84, 89-
91, 97, 103, 110, 113
Austria 90
France 154, 155
Netherlands 199-201
Portugal 90-1
Spain 91
United Kingdom 218-20
legislation enables 73-5, 80, 112
nature of 9, 53-62, 110
needs assessment 64, 79-80, 101,
103, 105-7, 110, 114, 116, 135,
155
operational innovation 60, 61,
99-107, 111, 114-15
organisational context 57-9,
100*fig*
organisational innovation 60, 61,
83-97, 111, 113-14, 115
pilot programmes 64-7, 81, 111
social context 9, 11-18
'step-models' 103-4, 104-5,
181-3, 202-3, 212-13, 214-17
strategic innovation 60, 61,
63-81, 111-12, 115
targeting of services 5, 83, 84,
86, 87-9
target groups *see* homeless
people
user involvement 23-4, 54, 71,
99, 100, 101-2, 106, 114
see also reintegration; structure
and agency; 'supported
housing'
integration *see* reintegration
Ireland
approaches to homelessness
71-2, 80, 90, 184-7
Child Care Act (1991) 38, 71, 80
data sources 5-6, 80
Homeless Initiative, Dublin
Region 71-2, 184-7

V

Vlaams Overleg Bewonersbelangen
(VOB), Belgium 68
voluntary agencies *see* non-
governmental organisations
Vranken, Jan 3, 56

W

Walenburg, Netherlands 103–4,
202–3
Walker, A. 99–100, 107
Watson, S. 3
welfare services
benefits 28, 30, 40–1, 44, 45–6
changes in 9–10, 15–18, 21–2, 24,
28
'in crisis' 16–18
participatory welfare 23–4
responsibility for homeless 49
welfare state regimes 10, 11–13,
14*fig*, 19, 20–1, 29–46, 54, 110
Wernham House, United Kingdom
96, 221–3
Wilhelmsdorf shelter *see* Wohnung
statt Heimplatz
Wohnplatform Linz, Austria 70, 90,
123–6
Wohnung statt Heimplatz,
Germany 86, 106, 171–5
Wunnengshellef, Luxembourg 73,
76–7, 101–2, 193–8

Y

Y-Foundation Supported Housing
Project, Finland 48–9, 68–9, 80,
86, 92, 94, 150–3

Z

Zaragoza City – Multiple Projects,
Spain 86–7, 89, 210–13

Other related titles from The Policy Press include:

Home Sweet Home? The impact of poor housing on health (1999: forthcoming)
Alex Marsh, David Gordon, Christina Pantazis and Pauline Heslop
ISBN 1 86134 176 8 £16.99 tbc pbk

Homelessness: Exploring the new terrain (1999: forthcoming)
Edited by Patricia Kennett and Alex Marsh
ISBN 1 86134 150 4 £18.99 pbk
ISBN 1 86134 167 9 £45.00 hdbk

Not mad, bad or young enough: Helping young homeless people with mental health problems (1999)
Lynn Watson
ISBN 1 86134 145 8 £11.95 pbk

Begging and street-level economic activity [tbc] (1999: forthcoming)
Edited by Hartley Dean
ISBN 1 86134 155 5 £18.99 pbk
ISBN 1 86134 178 4 £45.00 hdbk

In search of a home: An evaluation of refugee housing advice and development workers (1998)
Robin Means and Azra Sangster
ISBN 1 86134 095 8 £11.95

Managing to survive: Asylum seekers, refugees and access to social housing (1999)
Roger Zetter and Martyn Pearl
ISBN 1 86134 171 7 £14.99

Almshouses into the next millennium: Paternalism, partnership, progress? (1999)
Jenny Pannell with Caroline Thomas
ISBN 1 86134 164 4 £14.99

New poverty series edited by David Gordon
Studies in poverty, inequality and social exclusion

Tackling inequalities: Where are we now and what can be done?
Christina Pantazis and David Gordon
ISBN 1 86134 146 6 £15.99 pbk

The widening gap: Health inequalities and policy in Britain
Mary Shaw, Daniel Dorling, David Gordon and George Davey Smith
ISBN 1 86134 142 3 £14.99 pbk

Inequalities in health: The evidence
The evidence presented to the Independent Inquiry into Inequalities in
Health, chaired by Sir Donald Acheson
Edited by David Gordon
ISBN 1 86134 174 1 £16.99 pbk

All the above titles are available from
Biblios Publishers' Distribution Services Ltd
Star Road, Partridge Green, West Sussex RH13 8LD, UK
Telephone +44 (0)1403 710851, Fax +44 (0)1403 711143